D1192228

THE THEOLOGY OF POLITICS

The THEOLOGY *of* POLITICS

by
NATHANIEL MICKLEM
Principal of Mansfield College, Oxford

OXFORD UNIVERSITY PRESS
LONDON NEW YORK TORONTO
1941

OXFORD UNIVERSITY PRESS
AMEN HOUSE, E.C.4
London Edinburgh Glasgow New York
Toronto Melbourne Capetown Bombay
Calcutta Madras
HUMPHREY MILFORD
PUBLISHER TO THE UNIVERSITY

Printed in Great Britain

Nathaniel, Roberto, Ambrosio.

Vobis filiolis faustum det cernere mundum,
Provida quem simulat pagina nostra, deus.

CONTENTS

PREFACE

IN the homogeneous but unsystematic essays that compose this book I have not attempted the part of prophet or statesman, professional philosopher or theologian. I have written nothing learned or original or technical. I am a plagiarist, a popularizer, one of the *epigoni:*

dicitque mihi mea pagina, fur es.

I seem to myself to fall under the condemnation of Tristram Shandy as one of those who 'for ever make new books, as apothecaries make new mixtures, by pouring only out of one vessel into another', and who are 'for ever twisting and untwisting the same rope'.

My excuse is that the simple principles which this book expounds are of urgent relevance at the present turn of history, and that, not being new in themselves, they may come as new to some who read what I have written; for, if these principles are to some extent 'in our blood', they have in recent years been little in our minds.

Speaking in the House of Commons on 8th October 1940, Mr. Winston Churchill made reference to 'Christendom' as that which 'though now sundered by fearful quarrels and under the obsession of fearful tyrannies, constitutes the goal towards which we are marching and will march across the battlefields of the land, the sea and the air'. My purpose in this book is to elucidate the idea of 'Christendom'. Mr. Churchill is a statesman, not a theologian or sentimentalist. By 'Christendom', therefore, he means something realizable upon the stage of history; it is the ideal of the politician; on the other hand, it is somehow connected with religion. This book, therefore, is not a theological treatise, but it surveys the intermediate country between theology and politics, and it enforces the truth that, for better or for worse, our political philosophy, explicitly or implicitly, rests upon our theology.

All political problems are at bottom theological. It is true that the religious or irreligious labels that men wear offer no certain clue to their political opinions, but obviously a man's political outlook is coloured or even determined by his real thought, or thoughtlessness, about God and man and the meaning of human life.

Communism, as it has been developed in Russia, rests upon the presupposition that there is no God. Hence the individual soul or person is of no intrinsic value; hence the chilling doctrine of 'collective man' and the subordination of the individual to the State. The political life of National Socialism likewise rests upon doctrines or dogmas that are not in themselves political. Its roots lie in 'the seething soul of the German People' (*die kochende Volksseele*); its prophet and Messiah are to be detected beneath the not wholly Teutonic features of Herr Hitler; a disappointingly inferior German is the language of its revelation; it explicitly denies the Christian doctrine of God as the equal Father of all men with his transcendent and impartial law of justice.

Great Britain and America, on the other hand, show at first sight an astonishing indifference to religion. Since, then, religious convictions appear to enter so little into our political enthusiasms, and the moral judgements of society are not recognized as having any supernatural origin, it is tempting to suppose that the cause of liberty, of democracy, of civilization, as we value these, has little to do with religion, and that the variegated persuasions of Christian sects are of no political moment. But such would be an undiscerning judgement. The peoples of Great Britain and North America have been living for more than a generation upon inherited religious capital. Moral insights, severed from their roots in dogma, linger for a while as ethical conventions. But how insecure apart from dogma is that spiritual valuation of man upon which democracy rests may be inferred from a notice posted not long since in an American factory, 'Don't waste the time of the machine'.

Every conceivable political theory rests upon an implicit anthropology, a theological or anti-theological estimate of man as related to his God, to his fellows and to machines. 'Stalin', I read, 'destroyed some sixteen million horses, in order that the peasantry should be dependent on mechanized farming, and on machines the individual peasant can never hope to own.' That illustrates the application of economic theory to politics, but it is unthinkable apart from an implicit anthropology—and perhaps an hippology as well. If man is not made 'in the image of God', and horses have no claim on our gratitude and affection, by all means 'don't waste the time of the machine'.

The politician who surveys the world, therefore, will be more concerned with what men and women believe than with those transitory events which make 'sensational' headlines, but the issues of which depend so largely upon the response they evoke from human minds; he will take knowledge from the German example that what he regards as the fundamentals of civilized life, the common decencies of human behaviour, are insecure if a people take up with some new theology.

The breakdown of the League of Nations was due to the intractable prejudices and infirmities of men and nations. Its reason was at bottom theological. There cannot be an organized world-society except upon the basis of a common ethic, a common anthropology. The League and Covenant, far more than was realized by Europeans at the time, presupposed the traditions and principles of 'Christian' civilization. It is well understood that no nation in fact conducts its affairs in a noticeably Christian fashion; but Japan's invasion of China and, not less, her attempt to debauch the Chinese by unlimited opium; Italy's onslaught on Abyssinia and use of poison gas against the Abysinnians; Russia's repudiation of traditional ethics as bourgeois and as of no binding validity; Germany's assertion of a new ethic based upon the immanent urges of the German soul; and the genuine, if sometimes hesitant, concern for freedom and old-fashioned ideas of law and justice in other countries that inherit the traditions of Christendom—these together make impossible and absurd the idea of any far-reaching co-operative association of the nations. The military defeat of Germany in the present war may prove no impossible task, but the political problems of a post-war settlement rest upon problems that are not political but metaphysical, theological and religious.

There is a *philosophia perennis*, an abiding wisdom, a body of sound principles, which comes to us through Plato and Aristotle and Cicero and St. Augustine and St. Thomas Aquinas. On its political side it is the background and presupposition of our civilization in the West. It belongs to the sphere of Reason rather than of Revelation. But we must distinguish between Reason and mere logic. Both Marxism and National Socialism are logical systems, but they are fundamentally irrational because they rest rather upon passion than upon a quiet and sober reason which does justice to all the intuitions and intimations of the human spirit. The conception of man, of society and of the State set forth in these pages claims to be strictly rational; it owes as much to Hellenism as to any distinctively Christian source. It is human or humane; it is sober common sense.

But reason and common sense are not in themselves sufficient for our need. No political or economic theory is likely to affect deeply the conduct or outlook of man, unless it be allied to religion or a pseudo-religion of some sort. An economic materialism that denies the idea of God, that gives no abiding value to human life, and that represents history as the unfolding of inexorable laws could not in logic evoke in man any strenuous activity. But in fact the Communist ideal has kindled in the young of this generation a boundless enthusiasm and has carried many to heroic sacrifice. Atheist Communism, in despite of logic and to the vast inconvenience of well-established political parties, has become a pseudo-religion. Not as a political or economic theory but as a religion it compels the devotion of its adherents. National Socialism is likewise a religion. 'For us', says the egregious Dr. Ley, 'there is only one idea, one outlook, one life, one religion which can bring bliss—and that is the eternal belief in the German *Volk*, in its blood and in its soil and in its Creator. Our religion would not exist if our blood did not exist.'

It is precisely at this point that the democracies stand at a disadvantage. What is their religion? When Mr. Gladstone led the hosts of Nonconformity to the polls for social reform or thundered about Bulgarian atrocities, political action and enthusiasm were fed by religious conviction. 'The Nonconformist conscience' was a power in politics; it influenced the Cabinet; it made political freedom a cause to kindle the passionate enthusiasm of men and lift them above sectional and personal interest. But the Church counts for little in politics to-day. Governments, says Bishop Hensley Henson, 'now have no need to "tune" the pulpits: they get better results by "inspiring" the newspapers'. Sir Alfred Zimmern has shown how the Church after the last war largely identified itself with the cause of the League of Nations to the great confusion of politics while the alliance lasted and to the great prejudice of religion when the dream was broken.

It is part of the general secularism of the age that the Church, falling victim like the Marxists to a this-worldly millenarianism, put its money on the League. Against Herr Hitler and his gang the League was not even a starter, and the Christians, having been talking League of Nations for twenty years, have lost their political influence with their political message. There is much private and individual religion in the democracies, but the cause for which we now claim to be fighting no longer rests upon any religious basis.

Without the force of religion the politicians are largely impotent. Negatively, Great Britain is united in an excellent moral indignation that springs from the vestigial remains of the Christian outlook; but our pre-war social and political order does not kindle our loyalty or our enthusiasm; there is too much truth in Herr Hitler's taunts at our 'plutocracy'. In fighting for a new Europe, we are fighting for a new Britain also. Vaguely and inarticulately we long for 'Christendom'. Mere dislike of 'Hitlerism', however creditable, is insufficient. The Fascist and Communist experiments are violent and irrational attempts to remedy the undeniable defects and 'open sores' of capitalist democracy. We need an articulated philosophy of the State and of society, more rational, more attractive, more human than that of our enemies, and we need the impulse of religious conviction at least as passionately held as the pseudo-religions of Germany and Russia. Such a philosophy and such a religion are not to be found except in the Christian faith.

There are those who regard all social progress as an emancipation from the fetters laid upon the minds and activities of men by the Christian Church in centuries past. Such a contention cannot be answered by an epigram. Regarded as a human institution the Church has a sorry record of compromise, of blindness and of lethargy. The example of Christ is the judgement of the Church, and in various political movements outside the Church it is legitimate to see the appeal, whether conscious or unconscious, from the Church to the Spirit of Christ. It remains true, however, that all social and political advance comes through a fuller realization of principles implicit in Christ's teaching, with which the Church has been entrusted, and of which in the person of her saints she has been in fact the guardian.

All political problems are at bottom theological. No political theory is likely to affect deeply the conduct or outlook of man unless it be reinforced by the sanctions of religion. Thus my purpose is to indicate the outlines of a doctrine of society which makes its appeal to the reason and conscience of humane and civilized men but is also an effective answer to Marxist materialism and Nazi racialism because that which is consonant with reason may be apprehended as the will of the living God revealed in the teaching of Jesus Christ.

Some of the essays in this book have a literary history or genealogy. A few paragraphs from the Preface are transcribed from the 'Dr. Williamson' lecture which I had the honour to deliver before the Presbyterian College of Carmarthen in 1939. The essay on Marxism is based on a series of papers which appeared some months ago in the *British Weekly*; the chapter on Nazism does not greatly differ in substance from my broadcast 'talks' on the same theme. I am grateful to editors and proprietors for allowing me to plagiarize from myself as I have freely plagiarized from others. My dear and honoured friend, Hastings Rashdall, later Dean of Carlisle, first instructed me in the philosophy of politics, but my most direct guidance and inspiration I owe to my friend, Dr. Heinrich Rommen, now, I am thankful to say, a teacher at St. Joseph's College in Connecticut; if I have but rarely quoted from him, I am conscious of my debt to him from the first page to the last. My wife has lightened and dulcified my labours at the Index.

N. M.

MANSFIELD COLLEGE, OXFORD,
1941.

I

REFLECTIONS ON COMMUNISM

φημὶ γὰρ ἐγὼ εἶναι τὸ δίκαιον οὐκ ἄλλο τι ἢ τὸ τοῦ κρείττονος συμφέρον.

By the Church-going public and by all citizens who aspire to solidity Communism is regarded as a horrid nightmare of the Russian mind, a manifestation of Anti-Christ, and, so far as Great Britain is concerned, a bogy. But for better or for worse the Russian Revolution has been one of the decisive events of this century. Like the French Revolution it has profoundly influenced even those other countries that have endured its horrors only in the form of pamphlets.

The Communist Party in Great Britain at the present moment may be microscopic; but it is not so long since the Labour Party looked equally insignificant. There is no immediate likelihood that our lamp-posts will be decorated and diversified by swinging capitalists and pendent parsons; we are nursing, so far as we know, no Lenin in our British bosom; the 'anti-God Movement' makes little headway here. But Communism works like a fever in the veins of the youthful and the eager. A generation ago Herbert Spencer was 'all the rage'; now it is Karl Marx. Neither was a philosopher of merit, but we must understand them if we would understand our time; we must make our reckoning with Marx and Spencer. In particular, the power of Communism 'to communicate the will to serve, its sense of exhilaration through contact with high purpose, its ability to make all alien from itself seem mean and unimportant, these, certainly, are beyond discussion. It gives something of the mental and moral excitement that is felt by the reader of the poetry inspired by the French Revolution, the unconquerable hope, the heedless and instinctive generosity, which makes great ends seem worth working for because they are attainable by ourselves.' I am sure that when Professor Laski wrote those words, he had in mind the students of the London School of Economics not less than the youth of Russia. Vodka is an innocuous beverage compared to the heady fumes of Russian sociology.

It is therefore most necessary that we seek to understand this Communism. Yet how forbidding a task it is! Text-books of Marxist philosophy are not monuments of literary charm. Even the *Communist Manifesto* itself seems drab and faded to those familiar with the *Magnificat*; and the stoutest heart might well quail in the presence of *Das Kapital*. None the less, there are eager circles throughout the country that do study *Das Kapital* and appear to suck refreshment from it, and we must not hesitate to press upon our philosophers and theologians a task that to the commonalty of us might seem superhuman. If they would really help us in our present quandary, let them, very temporarily, lay aside Plato and the poets and the Bible, and study the literature of Communism.

This scientific task is altogether beyond my powers. I cannot expound or safely criticize the economics of Karl Marx; but I have attempted, as any man may, to understand Communism as a *Weltanschauung* or general 'philosophy of life' and to appreciate what is that in it which, in spite of the cynical invasion of Finland and the atrocities of tyranny in Russia, appeals to the imagination and kindles the generous emotions of the young. Which of us, indeed, gifted with any imagination has not revolted against the 'placidity emetical' of the prosperous and pious classes at the lot of the unemployed these past many years and at the appalling conditions of hunger, insecurity and squalor under which millions in this country have been living? We have wondered with Mr. T. S. Eliot, 'was our society, which had always been so assured of its superiority and rectitude, so confident of its unexamined premisses, assembled round anything more permanent than a congeries of banks, insurance companies, and industries, and had it any beliefs more essential than a belief in compound interest and the maintenance of dividends?' We will very gladly go to school with Karl Marx and with Comrade Lenin, if these can even hint to us of a better way.

I

The influence of Karl Marx has not been due to his winning manner, his irresistible charm or 'the insinuating subtlety of his carriage'. He has put a spell upon men, but not by eloquence, by any appeal to sentiment or by playing to the gallery. He was a rationalist, impatient of emotion, incapable of compromise, intolerant of opposition, an heroic but not an alluring figure. He suffered exile, neglect, vilification and protracted, bitter poverty. He loved his family and his friend Engels, but hatred rather than amiability marked his course. He did not even love the working class whose interests he sought with the selfless, abandoned, life-long devotion of a saint. It was a system rather than men that he hated, but men must be ruthlessly sacrificed if the cause demand it. He was a demonic figure.

Not for nothing has Mr. D. R. Davies called him 'the last of the Hebrew prophets'. He was prophetic not in the sense that he foresaw the future—for his predictions have been largely falsified by events—but in the sense that he revealed the present. In the eighth century before Christ the authorities in Northern Israel were reasonably well satisfied with the statistics of Church attendance and the popular support of religious rites; they took great pride in the advances of civilization and in the indications of a new prosperity as evidenced in palatial buildings and elaborate and tasteful gardens; taxation, no doubt, was high, but the country could stand it. Israel was prosperous and, as any one could see, it was religious. Better still, all this was but the prelude to that bright 'Day of the Lord' which would bring a new era to the earth. It was, in fact, the Victorian age of Israel's history. Then it fell to the prophet Amos to explain what all this was worth. 'Forasmuch, therefore, as your treading is upon the poor, and ye take from him burdens of wheat; ye have built houses of hewn stone, but ye shall not dwell in them; ye have planted pleasant vineyards, but ye shall not drink the wine of them. . . . They afflict the just, they take a bribe, and they turn aside the poor in the gate from their right. . . . I hate, I despise, your feast-days, and I will not smell in your solemn assemblies. . . . Take thou away from me the noise of thy songs; for I will not hear the melody of thy viols. But let judgement run down as waters, and righteousness as a mighty stream.' It was precisely this which in a secular idiom Karl Marx said to the Victorian age, and the thunder of his words still reverberates in the consciences of men.

That a terrific denunciation of the alleged wrongs of men should appeal mightily to the aggrieved is natural enough. It is more important that, however unsatisfactory are Marx's economics, however misguided and perverse many of his ideas, however reprehensible his policy, fundamentally his analysis of social ills was true.

'The history of all human society', we read at the bebinning of the *Communist Manifesto*, 'has been the history of class struggles.' We are very unwilling to admit that in free and democratic Britain the 'class-war' is a reality. Class distinctions, we say, are rapidly disappearing in this country, and there is much active good-will between the various sections of the people; duchesses go slumming, and men from the humbler classes achieve coronets. But this does not affect the substance of Karl Marx's contention.

Well-paid artisans may earn more than the vicar of their parish; many a working man may own his cottage or have something put away in the Post Office and thus qualify as a minor capitalist; the life of the financier may be more hazardous and repellent than that of the Corporation dustman; there may be much personal good-will between the classes; but there is a contrariety of interest inherent in our economic system. 'The modern State authority', says the *Communist Manifesto*, 'is nothing more than a committee for the administration of the common affairs of the bourgeois class as a whole.' Mr. T. S. Eliot hints at much the same: 'defenders of the totalitarian system can make out a plausible case for maintaining that what we have is not democracy, but financial oligarchy'.

Within living memory the squires and landlords have gone down before the rising power of the industrial grandees; they are no longer 'the governing class'. As there was an inevitable struggle for power between the landed interest and the *bourgeoisie*, so, it is said, there is inevitable enmity between the *bourgeoisie* and the proletariat; for our present order, political, economic and imperial, is conceived in the interests of the former. The class-struggle, says Marx, in spite of all palliatives of personal good-will, is an undeniable and inevitable fact, for the interests of the two classes are radically opposed. 'The wage-earners as a class are concerned only with securing the highest possible price for their labour, while the capitalists, again, as a class, are constrained, in the interests of profits, to purchase it at the minimum price.' Thus the contention is succinctly put by Professor Laski. It represents a fundamental fact of our present economic order. As a wage-earner my chief interest is high wages and economic security; as a capitalist my chief interest is profits. As a prudent capitalist I may think it pays me to offer higher wages than the minimum in order to keep the workmen fit and contented with their lot. As a Christian or humanitarian I may be willing and even eager to share with them some of my profits. But in general the first business of a company is to show profits, and the lower the wages-bill the higher the profits.

Moreover—this is Marx's contention—law, political and social life, imperial policy, morality and even religion in any epoch are but the shadow cast by the basic economic structure of society and the struggle of contending interests. This is very much the view which Plato long ago put into the mouth of his Thrasymachus: 'The different forms of government make laws democratical, aristocratical, tyrannical, with a view to their several interests, and these laws, which are made by them for their own interests, are the justice which they deliver to their subjects, and him who transgresses them they punish as a breaker of the law, and unjust. And that is what I mean when I say that in all states there is the same principle of justice, which is the interest of the government; and as the government must be supposed to have power, the only reasonable conclusion is, that everywhere there is one principle of justice, which is the interest of the stronger.'

A case can be made for this depressing view. A modern example may be cited from the sphere of law. The children of the well-to-do, for instance, afford an almost avuncular status to the policeman on his beat. Not so the children of the poor, and this not because the poor are really more wicked than the rich, but because it is the policeman's duty to punish them for doing things which do not seem to them wicked—such as 'pinching' a loaf of bread when they are very hungry—but it is not his duty to restrain landlords and employers from acts of injustice which seem to them—and would have seemed to 'the divine missionary of the New Testament'—fifty times more heinous. Again, a long and uphill fight was necessary in Great Britain to mitigate the cruel laws against wrongs done to property—with their pitiful sanctions of prison, transportation, death—while we have had to agitate and struggle to get any laws at all against child-labour, sweated industry and bad conditions for the workers.

Once more, the political freedom of democracy, it is said, arises and corresponds with the needs of the *bourgeoisie* victorious over old restrictions. Meanwhile the working man, beautifully free to vote but not in a position to decide upon what he will vote, and being the victim of grievous economic insecurity, has actually little more freedom than a villein in old days. Political freedom without economic freedom represents and perpetuates the domination of the bourgeois class.

'Of course the bourgeois family will disappear,' says the *Communist Manifesto*. Karl Marx was happily married and a devoted father. I cannot think that he advocated the annihilation or 'liquidation' of all family life. 'The bourgeois family', I imagine, connoted 'nannies' and nursemaids, governesses and school-rooms, gardens and stables and grooms, ponies and peacocks, fashionable 'prep. schools' and expensive secondary schools curiously called 'public' and dedicated to the training of a governing class. Since Marx's time there has been a revolutionary change in the size and equipment of the bourgeois family and in the democratizing of the nation's educational system. It is doubtful whether private schools will survive this present war. But in the past, England has had a class education which illustrated and exacerbated the 'class-war'.

Finally, colonial and imperial policy, qualified by Foreign Missions, 'forces all the nations' (I quote the *Communist Manifesto* again), 'under pain of extinction, to adopt the capitalist method of production; it constrains them to accept what is called civilization, to become bourgeois themselves'. Our expressed concern for 'native welfare' is always subject to the 'economic necessities' of the Western world.

The critics of the prophets will, no doubt, find much here to dispute and much to qualify; the insufficiencies of the theory appear more glaring as they are applied to morals and to religion; and it may be held that the Communist remedy is more painful and more perilous than the disease itself. But in broad outline Marx's analysis is true. The relatively well-to-do classes have not realized the extent to which our present order of society represents their own point of view and is subservient to their interests. They have sought to ameliorate by charity and good-will a system which, because its fundamental basis is sectional, is fundamentally unjust. The class struggle goes very deep. There is a rift, an estrangement, in our national life due to diversity of economic interest. It can be, and it must be, overcome. Of all internal political and economic problems this is the most urgent. Marxism has made us realize an open sore in the body politic or body economic. Whether we deal with it, once we see it, is, as regards the privileged classes, a plain moral issue.

II

A disquieting story which I read many years ago gave the experience of an eager but infelicitous evangelist. He was addressing a gathering of the very poor; their clothes were ragged, their hunger was unsated, and their dwellings were insanitary and verminous. The preacher bade them be cheerful and patient in the bright hope of a better world to come; for a season their lot might be distressing, but they might confidently look for 'a crown hereafter'. At this point a querulous voice inquired whether the speaker could not oblige with ''alf a crown now to be getting on with'. This anecdote hints at one of the sources of Communist atheism. Karl Marx was a man with little sense for religion, and in his later years no interest in it. Lenin knew religion—and that from the outside—only in the form of the Orthodox Church of Russia. Even in Great Britain and America religion has often been deemed an excellent bromide for keeping the working classes quiet, and John Wesley has been praised not least because he saved his country from violent revolution.

Eduard Bernstein thus expounds the Marxist view. 'The material basis of life, the manner in which life and its requirements are produced, determines in the last instance the social ideas and institutions of the time or historical epoch, so that fundamental changes in the former produce in the long run fundamental changes in the latter.' Morality and organized religion are amongst the social ideas and institutions of any period. Therefore any revolutionary change in the economic order will in time produce a parallel change in ideas of morality and of religion.

Up to a point this principle corresponds with fact. Apart from the *illuminati* of our own time the Christian Church has always found in the Holy Scriptures its unchanging standard and rule of faith and practice, but we shall not wisely dispute that there is a certain correspondence between social conditions and current theology, nor that Christian morality has been in fact accommodated to economic changes. A purely penal theory of the Atonement, for instance, cannot for long be maintained when even the secular courts regard punishment as being, at least in part, remedial. We may suspect, too, that the rise of Capitalism rather than increased ethical vision led to the abandonment of medieval strictures upon usury. To be sure, it is easier to argue that Calvinism produced Capitalism than vice versa, and Marx's almost exclusive emphasis upon the economic factor in the shaping of history is untenable, but the great influence of the economic situation upon Christian thought and conduct from age to age is matter for research, not for denial.

Indeed, a living religion must rightly and inevitably adapt itself to changing circumstance. This is a theme of *A Clue to History* by Professor John Macmurray, who has been much influenced by the theory of knowledge propounded in Communist philosophy. He finds the continuity of Christianity through all its changes in an abiding identity of 'intention' to realize the will of God as made known in Christ. A man striving after an ideal, he urges, may discover that he has chosen the wrong means, and therefore change his course of action without changing his intention, and, as life goes on, he may attain an ever deeper insight into that intention which he apprehended but dimly as a youth. Thus the Church's 'intention' remains identical through all developments of theology or economic change.

But even this does not fully meet the Communist contention. 'All contemporary religions and churches,' said Lenin, 'all and every kind of religious organizations Marxism has always viewed as organs of bourgeois reaction, serving as a defence of exploitation and doping the working class.' Religion, as another apologist for Marxism has said, 'gives supernatural sanction to every form of exploitation and violence. It certifies existing institutions as parts of an eternal, divine order. War, slavery, the factory system employing little children, poverty, even disease, have all been justified and even sanctioned by religion.'

The traditional observations of Nonconformists upon the political activities of bishops in the House of Lords would seem to bear this out; slavery has been defended out of Scripture even by the Nonconformists; our political and social liberties, such as they are, have generally been won against the entrenched resistance of the established Church. Of Roman Catholicism and Eastern Orthodoxy, in particular, we must say that rarely, if ever, has their influence been other than conservative, even in the defence of manifold and crying wrongs. Even to-day and in Great Britain the Church appears to many to be on the side of the established order and against the new world which eager and generous hearts desire. The Church appears as an eminent vested interest, a capitalist corporation on a gigantic scale.

But there is another side to the story. Slavery, once defended by the Church, was later abolished by the quickened Christian conscience. If political liberties and social reforms in England were achieved against the resistance of the established Church, they were also won chiefly through the influence and determination of the Christian Nonconformists. To-day the old gibe that the Church of England represents 'the Tory Party at prayer' has lost its point and sting. The Labour Party in England, especially in its earlier days, has been led by Christians and by those whose sympathy and enthusiasm have been kindled by the Gospels. To put the case at its lowest, there is no necessary connexion between religion and political reaction!

But, further, we may admit that morality tends to decay into convention, that organized Christianity has often defended the cause of the oppressor, and that to this day the Christians as a whole are strangely and unpardonably tolerant of monstrous social evils. But what the Christians practise is, and always has been, very different from what they preach. The cry of the economically or politically oppressed has been for that justice which religion has proclaimed, and the freedom demanded by reformers and revolutionaries has no meaning except upon the basis of a spiritual interpretation of human life. The altruistic enthusiasm that has inspired the Socialist movement in many of its phases and led to the selfless devotion of many who denied the right or reality of religion rests upon a contradiction. 'If the materialist view were taken strictly,' write two modern critics, 'which rarely happens in the case of men of Marx's moral calibre, life would resolve itself into a scramble for material goods, like that of pigs for the pig-wash; for the assertion that the other pig should have an equal amount of wash is a spiritual assertion. A low view of man leads to a short and petty view of life, but men who call upon their fellows for altruism and devotion and who are concerned about the just ordering of human affairs, as Marx manifestly was, are unconsciously and illogically acting on a higher and more spiritual view of life than they sometimes profess in their theories.' We might, indeed, apply to Marx the tribute offered by John Ruskin to J. S. Mill: 'He deserves honour amongst economists by inadvertently disclaiming the principles which he states, and tacitly introducing the moral considerations with which he declares his science has no connection. Many of his chapters are, therefore, true and valuable; and the only conclusions of his which I have to dispute are those which follow from his premises.' Why should not the legal owner of vast estates in Scotland eject the crofters from their homes in the interests of grouse? Why should not children be employed all day in factories if the parents consent and the children themselves make no complaint? Why should not Adolf Hitler drive Poles from their homes and send them off to freeze and starve in cattle trucks, or satisfy his perverted passions in the degradation of the Jews? There seems no answer to these questions except upon a spiritual view of man.

Of the *Communist Manifesto* it has been said that it is 'a serious disloyalty to its own real meaning that almost the only explicit recognition of the moral and spiritual interests at stake is contained in the following passage: "In bourgeois society capital is independent and personal, while the living individual is dependent and deprived of personality."' But is this curious phrase 'deprived of personality' truly an indication of the 'real meaning' of the manifesto, or is it, perhaps, an unintentional concession to 'bourgeois' ways of thought? This is one of the puzzles presented to our thought by Communism. It reappears again in Lenin's observation that the economic oppression of the workers 'renders the spiritual and moral life of the masses coarser and more sordid'. Is Communism really concerned about the rights of 'personality', about 'the spiritual and moral life of the masses'? If it is, the rulers of Russia have been grievously disloyal to their own creed. Without a qualm, it appears, Stalin will 'liquidate' thousands of human lives as a 'surgical operation'; and how can a system that regards the spiritual and moral life of man as a mere secretion thrown off by economic conditions really be concerned for the things of the spirit and of human character? Our human powers of self-deception seem quite unlimited; and Communism appeals to men to-day in the name of the rights of personality and of the spiritual and moral life of men, all of which it denies and destroys both in theory and practice.

III

There is, of course, strictly no theology of Marxism, for the Communists deny the existence of God and regard religion, not without reason, as one of their worst enemies. Yet, such is the religious incurability of man, there is a kind of pseudo-theology or substitute religion of the Communists.

Religion, they say, is an illusion, not a scientific 'ideology'; the idea of God is first a projection of desire and later a device for the oppression of the masses; religious notions are simply the reflection of economic conditions or of the prejudice of the governing class.

Of this Professor Laski offers a curious illustration: 'Not less significant is the history, between the Reformation and the Revolution of 1688, of the doctrine of toleration. Scattered thinkers like Robert Brown [*sic*], statesmen like William of Orange, were able to see its value; but to their own day it was a plea without either moral or intellectual validity. But, when in the seventeenth century it was found incompatible with commercial prosperity to persecute, men had no difficulty in affirming that a religion of love was incompatible with repression made in its name.' When one is concerned to make a fortune, it is, no doubt, monstrously inconvenient to have to pick one's customers by their religious views, and business advantage may very well have contributed to the hard-won victory of toleration. But was the rise of Capitalism more than a contributory cause? Robert Browne, the Separatist, was followed in time by the Gulielmus Brown of Winthrop Praed:

> And when religious sects ran mad,
> He held, in spite of all his learning,
> That, if a man's belief is bad,
> It will not be improved by burning.

Capitalism, one suspects, was no more influential in the one case than the other. 'The temple of Janus, with his two controversial faces, might now not insignificantly be set open. And, though all the winds of doctrine were let loose to play upon the earth, so truth be in the field, we do injuriously by licensing and prohibiting to misdoubt her strength. Let her and falsehood grapple; who ever knew truth put to the worse, in a free and open encounter?' I cannot think that Milton, when he penned these gallant words, was no more than the unconscious agent of big business, the distorted echo of some economic law.

The persecution of Jews, Christians, Poles, Czechs, scientists and men of culture generally by Adolf Hitler in the service of his racial theory is one of many indications that ideas are more potent than economic laws or business interests. 'It is not the consciousness of men that determines their existence', wrote Marx, 'but, on the contrary, their social existence determines their consciousness.' He himself, however, by the cataclysmic effect of his own writings, is sufficient refutation of his creed; for, as Mr. Berlin remarks, his writing 'set out to refute the proposition that ideas govern the course of history, but the very extent of its own influence on human affairs has weakened the force of its thesis'; his work 'remains the most powerful among the intellectual forces which are to-day permanently transforming the ways in which men think and act'.

When we ask our statesmen what are their war aims to-day, they are apt somewhat impatiently to tell us that their first aim is to win the war, and that they cannot prognosticate their policy for a world the conditions of which are unpredictable. Similarly, if we cross-question the Communist about his ultimate aims, he replies in effect: 'There is a war on, the final and desperate struggle for the emancipation of the enslaved; our one task is to win the war; we have no time to sketch Utopias for the future, and, besides, our mentality and our ideas will change with the routing of the enemy and the emergence of a new economic era. History is an active agency; it is for us to create the future, not to speculate about it.' We may not withhold our sympathy from the harassed fighter on the stricken field who has no time for vague idealisms. But, little as he realizes it, the Marxist himself falls victim to an idealism of a singularly unconvincing kind. In spite of his rationalism Karl Marx was a romantic believing that a veritable Messianic age must dawn when at last the Capitalist oppression is overthrown and the proletarian has lost his chains. Even Lenin could so far forget himself as to write of the 'struggle of the oppressed class to set up a heaven on earth'. The idea that man can set up heaven on earth is sentimental and Utopian. Sancho

Panza was wiser: 'every one is as God made him, and very often worse'.

A judicious friend, to whom I lent a book on French Syndicalism many years ago, returned it with the remark that the politicians make an even greater mistake than the theologians when they forget original sin. The Soviet Republics have achieved much, but human nature does not seem automatically to become more genial, more gentle or even more humane under the direction of a Lenin or a Stalin. The Communist might reply that what we call geniality, gentleness and humanity are mere bourgeois notions, the mannerisms of the well-to-do, arbitrary canons of goodness to keep the worker in his place; current morality is class morality; 'the ethic of the proletariat springs from its revolutionary aspirations; it is these which give it the greater part of its power and elevation', said Georges Sorel. But human nature has been found even by dictators to be intractable.

The ingenious American who wrote a book to prove that the Golden Rule is the pathway to success in business is a conspicuous example of the way in which morality can be perverted into the conventions of the possessing classes. But 'class morality' involves a contradiction. Morality has no meaning apart from a transcendent and unchanging law. Those who have been drawn to Communism by their generous emotions have not realized that it does not offer a new, unconventional morality but denies morality, properly so called, altogether. 'We deny all morality taken from superhuman or non-class conceptions,' wrote Lenin; 'we say that this is a deception, a swindle, a befogging of the minds of the workers and peasants in the interests of the landlords and capitalists. We say that our morality is wholly subordinated to the interests of the class struggle of the proletariat.' This is strictly not morality at all, and the use of the term is either a relapse into bourgeois ways of thinking or an implicit contradiction. For Karl Marx, says Mr. Berlin, 'all notions of right and wrong, justice and injustice, altruism and egoism were beside the point, as referring exclusively to the mental states which, in themselves quite genuine, were never more than symptoms of the actual condition of their owner'. Again, 'phrases about justice or liberty represent something more or less definite when they are uttered by the middle-class Liberal, namely, his attitude to his own mode of life, his actual or sought-for relation to members of other social classes. But they are empty sounds when repeated by the proletarians, since they describe nothing real in his life and only betray his muddled state of mind, the result of the hypnotic power of phrases which, by confusing issues, not only fail to promote, but hinder and sometimes paralyse his power to act.'

Inevitably, therefore, the good Communist takes up with atheism. Religion means an eternal law of right and wrong, inexorable and indefectible, a justice that our present order so largely denies, that sanctions, indeed, the indignation of the oppressed but condemns the whole policy of the Communist revolution. Our present order may be but a bourgeois travesty of justice, but let justice, as we preach but do not practise it, be dubbed a transient convention, and let the norm of proper conduct become the immanent urges of the racial soul as in Nazi Germany or the emergent demands of the proletarian victors as in Russia, and right and wrong, as Marx saw, have lost their meaning, and any iniquity of persecution, of spoliation, of torture and mass-murder may be condoned and even praised. A movement that issued forth under the fair name of justice ends by denying that in justice there is any meaning; a movement that started under the banner of freedom ends in slavery, because it has repudiated the only sure foundation of human freedom, the spiritual conception of man as a potential child of God.

I have tried to show, first, that Karl Marx rightly

diagnosed the inevitable tension in our present order between those whose interest must be high wages and those whose interest is to keep down the wages-bill, and that the well-to-do and the religious have been both blind and complacent about grievous social wrongs; second, that there is not, as the Marxists have supposed, a necessary connexion between religion and political reaction; third, that Marxism, in spite of its denials, is Utopian in outlook, and by its religious negations destroys the foundations of that freedom and justice which it often claims to serve. I must finally consider the Red Revolution.

IV

'Communists never demean themselves to dissemble their opinions and their aims. They openly proclaim that their ends can be gained only by the violent subversion of the whole traditional social order.' This I have received as a quotation from the 1936 edition of the official *Programme of the Communist International*. 'The Communist parties', to quote another official publication, 'enrol only those who are firmly resolved to employ all their energies in tireless preparation for armed insurrection to destroy capitalism.'

Communists contend that 'Social Reform' is like a pill to cure an earthquake, that the propertied classes will never voluntarily relinquish privilege, that all man's social woes are due to Capitalism and exploitation, that the existing, if latent, class war must be exacerbated, and that by strikes, by tampering with the loyalty of the Army, by the preparation of plans and the storage of arms a situation must be created where the Communist party in the name of the workers of the world can seize the machinery of the State and 'liquidate' all opposition.

Even a country that is normally divided by faction tends to unity in the face of a common peril. Unless I have entirely misunderstood such Communist literature as I have seen, the Communist will welcome this war and actively hope for his nation's defeat, since this will facilitate chaos and the 'dictatorship of the proletariat'; all wars, even that on which we are now engaged, are due to 'imperialism', as Lenin used the term; the Communist has no sympathy with either side; he must do all he can to foster disaffection and disrupt national unity; he must work for chaos, that out of chaos, as in Russia, the Communist party may leap to the wheel of power.

Those who feel that their lives have been stunted, their homes ruined, their human rights denied by their economic status easily fall prey to blind anger, fierce jealousy and demonic hatred. In Neuberg's *Armed Insurrection* we may read: 'the masses must realize that they are going into a bloody and desperate armed struggle. . . . Their watchword must be attack, not defence; their objective, the pitiless extermination of the enemy,' and, again, 'street fighting, aiming at the physical extermination of the enemy should be absolutely without quarter. Any sign of human feeling from the proletariat to its class enemies during the armed struggle merely creates fresh difficulties. . . . The attack should be made by surprise, and all the leaders on the other side should first be assassinated, and all who might oppose the success of the undertaking exterminated.' The most interesting phrase in these dreadful passages is the curious reference to the suppression of 'human feeling'. Either this is another strange lapse into bourgeois ideas or it is an unintentional recognition of the iniquity of such a plan. I find it almost incredible that any of my fellow-countrymen should seriously favour and espouse this policy. But then I have found it almost incredible that the Germans, whom I have known and liked, should have provided enough perverts to staff Heinrich Himmler's *Gestapo*. Before the war there was a British Communist Party; it has never repudiated the way of

Moscow. It would be sentimental to suppose that Communists here or elsewhere are only trying to make our flesh creep when they talk of violence.

It is very plain that a revolution, which began in Russia with a massacre of the 'capitalists', has developed into a tyranny under which no man can trust his neighbour. Between May 1937 and the autumn of 1939, I read, '28 of the 68 candidates for the Central Committee of the Communist Party have been shot or have otherwise disappeared . . . nine out of 13 commissaries of the Russian Federal Republic have been arrested; eight out of 13 People's Commissaries of the Ukraine have been shot; and seven out of 13 People's Commissaries of White Russia have been either arrested or shot . . . 43 out of 53 secretaries of central Party organizations have been declared public enemies. Of 11 Presidents of the Council of People's Commissaries nine have been shot in the same period. Of the seven Presidents of the Central Executive Committee five have been declared public enemies. And of the 24 members of the original Central Committee only four retain their office.' In the same period, of the five marshals in the Army 'two have been executed, as have three out of the six Army Group Commanders, 10 of the 13 Army Commanders, 57 of the 85 Army Corps Commanders, 110 out of the 193 Divisional Commanders, and 202 out of 400 Brigade Commanders'. Let but the wicked 'capitalists' be 'liquidated' and their property confiscated, then the workers, 'who have nothing to lose but their chains', will live together in a classless condition of brotherhood and justice! The transformation of Russia by the Communists has been at the cost of a reign of terror which, twenty years and more after the Revolution, finds its victims amongst the classless workers.

It is hard to appraise the economic and political achievements of Soviet Russia; it is impossible to know what is happening in the souls of the Russian people. Russia stands in the public eye for militant atheism, for the destruction of European culture, for ruthless tyranny over soul and body. Even those who welcomed the revolution with most hope and sympathy are deeply disillusioned. But a merely negative attitude of revulsion or hatred is insufficient. The pre-war social and economic order of the democracies is not an answer to Bolshevism, but almost an excuse for it. Karl Marx's analysis of our economic ills remains; the Russian experiment may have been disastrous, but capitalistic individualism stands condemned. We must offer a better solution than that of the Russian Soviets, and we shall need sacrifice and devotion not less than that which overthrew the old régime of the Tsars and in a generation changed the face of Russia.

II

THE TOTALITARIANS

Ausi omnes immane nefas ausique potiti.

rursus prosperum ac felix scelus
Virtus vocatur; sortibus parent boni,
Jus est in armis, opprimit leges timor.

THE twin dictators of Italy and Germany are not well thought of in Great Britain. We regard them with contempt and 'savage indignation'. But our detestation of their ways should not blind us to the significance and appeal of the principles which they embody so unattractively. 'Fascism' or totalitarianism is not without its allurements for many in other lands. Its spiritual home may be Italy, but its superlative logical development has been in Germany. Its principles, therefore, may best be considered in their German guise. I will not retell the obscene horrors of Concentration Camps, Jew-baiting and government by the *Gestapo*, but will keep to certain underlying principles of permanent significance.

I

The Soviet Government of Russia stands for a materialist conception of history, the German Government for a racial. The Nazis maintain that the Aryan is the one creative race among mankind; it alone has been responsible for great art and great thought and great leadership; it is superior to all other races by nature, and it rules over them by right; the best and purest illustration of the

Aryan race is the German; therefore at all costs the German stock must be kept pure that it may fulfil its destiny to lead and inspire and rule the world.

'Certain well-marked differences of "national type"', says Professor Julian Huxley, 'are recognized in popular judgement—we all know the comic paper caricature of the Frenchman, the German, &c.—but it is very remarkable how personal and variable are such judgements. Thus our German neighbours have ascribed to themselves a Teutonic type that is fair, long-headed, tall, slender, unemotional, brave, straightforward, gentle and virile. Let us make a composite picture of a typical Teuton from the most prominent of the exponents of this view. Let him be physically as blond and mentally as unemotional as Hitler, physically as long-headed and mentally as direct as Rosenberg, as tall and truthful as Goebbels, as slender and gentle as Goering, and as manly and straightforward as Streicher. How much would he resemble the German ideal?' A correspondent in *The Times* pointed out that in 1938 the Nazis published a book with the biographies of the most famous two hundred 'Aryan' Germans from Gutenberg to Richtofen; these two hundred include four Poles, one Hungarian, ten Swiss, together with persons of Flemish, Moravian, English, Scottish, Swedish, Slavonic and Hungarian extraction!

It is not necessary to linger on the myth of the Aryans, for scientific research knows no such race. There is a group of Aryan languages which includes Latin, Greek, Sanskrit and Persian; the monumental work of von Schroeder on Aryan religion indicates that from the late Stone Age 'Aryans' have increasingly achieved higher spiritual vision than the present rulers of Germany. But if we add together the contributions made to human life and civilization by those who have spoken one of the cognate Aryan languages, and include the subtleties and insights of Greek literature, the laws and aqueducts of

Rome, the fervour of the Gathas, the boisterous humanity of the Edda, the naïve religion of the Rig-Veda, and add the scientific achievements of the 'white races' in recent years, no doubt the total is impressive. If we, further, give ourselves the advantage, which the Nazis have assumed, of deeming the Japanese to be honorary Aryans and of claiming the Person of Jesus Christ for the supposed Aryan race, the sum is almost overwhelming. Even so there are significant omissions such as Confucius and the authors of the Bible. But the whole theory is completely devoid of scientific worth and will appeal only to those who are seeking to think with their 'blood' instead of with their heads.

But behind the fantasies of the racial theory lies that sense of inherent superiority which the various peoples of the world are apt to enjoy when they contemplate their neighbours. The world at the moment is not in the mood to be amused by the German claim to spiritual and cultural superiority. But the Chinese, the Indians, the British and the Americans are in varying ways wont to regard with a certain pity the 'lesser breeds without the law' who inhabit less favoured countries and manage their affairs with variations of ineptitude. In theological terms this is the doctrine of election.

It seems in fact to be true that nations differ as much as individuals and that each has its peculiar gifts. This would be matter for unqualified satisfaction, since variety is the spice of life, were it not that certain races at certain times have conceived themselves to have the gift and therefore the duty and the destiny to mind the business of all the rest,

Parcere subjectis et debellare superbos.

The German claim to this gift is felt by the rest of the world to be insupportable; the British would never make such a claim, but, while they speak of their empire as acquired in sheer absence of mind, and congratulate themselves on a happy knack of colonial government, and pretend to groan under the white man's burden, they view the imperial map with considerable complacency and are disposed to see in it the hand of Providence. It is, therefore, not altogether surprising that Irishmen like Mr. G. B. Shaw and Russians like Lenin should suggest that all imperialisms are much alike. Happily the distinction between the German's claim and the Briton's disavowal is clearer to-day than heretofore. If a Briton cannot escape the conviction that those peoples are happy who live under the British flag, he recognizes that Colonial government is tutelage for freedom, and that the use of power for the exploiting of the weak is not permissible.

The conviction of its own superiority implanted in the bosom of each nation is an amiability, not an offence against philosophy, provided it be conjoined with a recognition that every other nation may properly cherish, however delusively, the same conviction about itself. The tulip, no doubt, fancies itself above the violet, but there is room for both in the garden. Germans of the Nazi persuasion, however, would reserve all sunny patches for themselves; all other peoples are deemed relatively servile; the negro is in Hitler's phrase 'half-ape'. The Nazis would not only rule the world but organize it, exploit it and stamp it with the upstart culture of Berlin. This claim is very naturally resented by other peoples; it is felt to be aesthetically revolting as well as politically uncomfortable; it is as if Beethoven and Bach were to be re-edited by Wagner, and Aristotle brought up to date by Alfred Rosenberg.

The claims of the Italians are less exorbitant. They speak of *mare nostrum* (though, as I write, their fleet does not venture upon its dangerous waters), but not yet have they laid claim to *orbis noster*. Yet in principle their *sacro egoismo* is not different from more blatant Teutonic pretensions.

II

In its more serious aspects, however, totalitarianism is a doctrine of the internal economy of a nation rather than of its relations to its neighbours. Here its strength and its appeal lie in its answer to the chaos of mob-democracy, to the hidden dominance of the lords of finance, 'to the social disruption of individualism, and to all the evils and wrongs of the "class-war".' It proclaims the indivisible unity and sacred destiny of the nation, and pays honour to the principle that the good of the body politic must have precedence over private gain; it calls to a sacrifice that it assures and a glory that it anticipates. It appeals to the idealists as well as to the victims of economic and political disorder.

But the price paid for these advantages is heavy. In his racialism the Nazi seems at the opposite pole from the international Marxist, but the Nazi conception of the individual is very close to the 'collective man' of Russian 'ideology'. Adolf Hitler has a withering contempt for the masses; Karl Marx counterbalanced his dreams of the proletariat by an engaging disrespect for proletarians. Both in Germany and in Russia a system organized for the benefit of all is wholly indifferent to the fate of each. Men in general are necessary that the blessings of the Nazi or Marxist régime may be enjoyed, but the individual has no value in himself. A low and unspiritual view of man is the prelude to inevitable slavery.

The Nazi State is constructed on the principles of the Prussian Army. Adolf Hitler says in *Mein Kampf*: 'the principle which once made the Prussian army the most wonderful instrument of the German nation must form . . . the basis of our State conception. Authority of each leader over those below him and, in turn, responsibility towards those above him.' The rigid discipline of the goose-stepping army is frankly the model for the State.

The theory has been drastically achieved in practice. The whole organization of the German nation is military. Not only is National Socialism itself a form of national mobilization, but also all the affairs of the nation—business, labour organization, the Press, education, music, the home and even religion—are organized by commissioned officers to be obeyed without question by the people.

Much of the staff work has been good. The economic organization of totalitarian States may in many respects be preferable to our own—but at the cost of freedom. In Germany no political opposition is allowed; no newspaper may increase its circulation by a criticism of the Government; all editors are given material which they are compelled to print, though they know, and their readers suspect, that it is false; no book disapproved by the Government may be printed or sold; no public meetings may be held by private causes; the police may at any time search houses, tamper with correspondence, listen-in on private telephones; the Secret Police, who are not subject to the Ministry of Justice, may arrest, detain and even torture and do to death without preferring any charge against their victim; their is no habeas corpus, no court of appeal from Party tyranny. Even the family is not safe from State interference; children may be taken from their parents, and brought up in institutions, if the parents' political opinions be suspect. There is reasonable security for the worker—provided he make no criticisms; but any expressed distaste for the Government, whether on political or religious grounds, is treasonable, and the Nazis have a short way with traitors. The whole State, even, in peace time, is, as it were, a department of the Prussian Army. Germany is strictly a servile State bent on enslaving its neighbours also.

Adolf Hitler despises the masses; his government is an oligarchy—of gangsters. The Nazi Party, he says, 'must not be the servant of the mass but its master'. 'The majority of the people is simple and gullible. . . . The State, therefore, must not allow itself to be induced by all the bragging about the so-called "freedom of the Press" to neglect its duty and deprive the nation of the mental food which it needs and which is good for it. With ruthless determination it must take over this means of mass education and use it in the service of the State and the nation.' Again, propaganda 'has not objectively to investigate the truth so far as it is favourable to the other side and to present it to the masses in doctrinaire honesty, but to serve its own truth unceasingly.'

'We begin with the child when he is three years old,' says Dr. Ley, the leader of the Nazi Labour Front; 'as soon as he begins to think, he gets a little flag put in his hand; then follows the school, the Hitler Youth, the Storm Troops and military training. We don't let him go; and, when adolescence is past, then comes the Labour Front which takes him again, and, whether he likes it or not, does not let him go until he dies.' What, then, are the children from the age of three to learn, what are the 'slogans' that are to be drilled into the thick heads of the stupid masses? That they serve God as they serve Germany, and that they serve Germany as they obey Adolf Hitler—blindfold; that a nation becomes great by war and flabby in peace; that the old-fashioned 'Christian' virtues, such as mercy, gentleness and love, are unworthy of German 'honour'. The idea of universal love, said Alfred Rosenberg, is 'a blow at the soul of Nordic Europe'. Boys must learn, first and foremost, to be soldiers, girls to bear children who may carry German arms. Germany stands high above other peoples of mixed race; therefore all foreign contamination must be avoided; only German ideas, German music, German art, German pictures may be safely cultivated; it is the task of Germans to subdue the world. In particular, the corrupter of nations, the parasite, the loathly 'bacillus', the Jew, with all his works, must be destroyed; humanitarianism, says Adolf Hitler, is 'a compound of stupidity, cowardice and arrogance'. Such is the stuff of Nazi education. There have been many tyrannies since the world began, but no such tyranny over the minds and souls of men, and none in the interests of a philosophy so crass and primitive.

In National Socialism we see worked out with inflexible logic two principles, to both of which in other lands also men are prone, first that one's own race, whichever it may be, is superior to all others and must organize them for their good, and second, that the individual exists only for the State. These principles can neither be disproved by the logicians nor accepted by the humane and the civilized. But the rejection of them implies that both men and nations have equal rights, though not equal gifts, and it is doubtful whether such a conviction has either foundation or stability apart from a belief in God as the Artificer of all nations and the equal Father of all men. National Socialism, Communism and competitive Capitalism combine to show that freedom is never safe apart from the religious valuation of man as a potential child of God.

III

The basis of freedom is the law, which is equal and available for all and is an expression of eternal justice. So we think, but here too the Nazi philosophy is logical. The destiny of Germany is to express the national 'soul' and to lead and dominate the world. This is the central theme of history. Whatever, therefore, serves this divinely ordered end is right, whatever thwarts it is wrong. But the demands of the German 'soul' and German destiny must be interpreted and defined; the organ of this revelation is obviously the Nazi Party which by its achievements and by its peculiar sensitivity to the

Germanic spirit may claim to speak for Germany. But Nazis like thieves fall out sometimes; therefore in the last resort the Leader to whom all the Nazis have sworn obedience is the final arbiter of the German 'soul', the interpreter of German destiny, the source of German law and German right. Law is the expression of Herr Hitler's will. It has no connexion, therefore (apart from the bandage round the eyes) with the figure of universal justice. It is a matter of little moment whether law be identified with the destiny of Germany as interpreted by the Nazi Party or with the advantage of the proletariat as interpreted by the Communist Party; in both cases law is an expression, not of reason and universal justice, but of human will and prejudice. *Sit pro ratione voluntas.*

A new German morality, therefore, has taken the place of human morality. Dr. Kraemer, a high legal authority among the Nazis, says, 'Justice is whatever is of benefit to the nation, whatever corresponds with the German feeling of justice, the unadulterated voice of God in the race-pure soul.' We are disposed to say that the rape of Czecho-Slovakia, the destruction in Rotterdam, the treatment of the Social Democrats and Jews in Germany are unjust; but this, we are told, is simply our flabby, democratic, liberalistic notion of justice; justice is whatever benefits the Germans; justice is whatever the *Volk* feels to be just. 'Right and just', said Herr Buerckel, one of Herr Hitler's chiefs, 'is in the end only what serves the nation and its preservation.' There is no universal justice in heaven, there is only Herr Hitler's justice upon earth. It was quite in character, therefore, that Captain Manfred, who had been involved in a political murder, was appointed President of the supreme Tribunal of the People, and that, as soon as he had invaded Austria, Herr Hitler put at the head of the Austrian police Herr Steinhäsl, one of the murderers of Dr. Dollfuss.

In his very impressive Encyclical, *Mit Brennender Sorge*,

the late Pope said: 'It is part of the trend of the day to sever more and more not only morality but also the foundation of law and jurisprudence from true belief in God and from His revealed commandments. Here we have in mind particularly the so-called natural law, that is written by the finger of the Creator Himself in the tables of the hearts of men and which can be read on these tables by sound reason not darkened by sin and passion. Every positive law, from whatever lawgiver it may come, can be examined as to its moral implications, and consequently as to its moral authority to bind in conscience, in the light of the commandments of the natural law. The laws of man which are in direct contradiction of the natural law bear an initial defect, that no violent means, no outward display of power, can remedy.'

IV

Another question which the National Socialist experiment has brought into relief is the place of religions and therewith of intellectual freedom in the State. Here the Nazis, less logical than elsewhere, maintain two principles. First, the task of religion is to strengthen the national morale. Herr Hitler would desire the parsons of his militarized nation to be like Army chaplains, who, as he thinks, have as their one duty to preach to the people 'for God and Hitler!' and to marshal the spiritual forces of the nation behind the Nazi policy. He has stated again and again that he has no quarrel with religion; he would gladly offer himself as patron and supporter of the Church—if only the Church would whole-heartedly commit itself to him.

The second principle is often set forth in the famous words of Frederick the Great, 'Any one may be saved in any way he likes', or, in other words, religion is a purely private matter with which the State and the Party have no desire to interfere. Herr Hitler has always maintained that religion in Germany is free and unrestricted. Religion, he says, is concerned with the world beyond, with spiritual aspirations, with pious feelings, with ideas about God and heaven. Let men follow their own bent in these speculations and enjoyments. Let the parsons confine their attention to the other world, but this world is the sphere of the politician; here the ideas of Herr Hitler must prevail. Thus there is no clash between religion and the State; let the parson get on with his supernatural interests, and let Herr Hitler manage this world's affairs. What could be fairer than that?

Were it not that the lion and the lamb have long since learned to lie down in amity together in the confused pasturage of the human mind, it would have been difficult to maintain simultaneously and with equal emphasis that the task of religion is to strengthen the national morale, and that its sphere is entirely other-worldly. But it is common to these else discordant views, that religion must not criticize, or interfere with, the Nazi Party. Herr Hitler would have liked one great national Church to support the Nazi revolution with the intensity and single-mindedness of religious fervour. 'One Reich, one Führer, one Church' has been a battle-cry. For this purpose little could be hoped from the Roman Church, internationally organized and owning an allegiance outside Germany. But an alluring prospect was dangled before the Protestants. Was not Luther a great German patriot? Had he not always supported the authority of the State? In this great hour of the nation's destiny let the sectional Protestant churches join into one, let them provide a channel for the fierce emotional enthusiasm of the Revolution; Herr Hitler would support them, befriend them, open for them the way to a spiritual chaplaincy to the regimented nation —'all this will I give thee, if only thou wilt bow down and worship me'. There has been no persecution of those

Christians who have acquiesced in these conditions; the rest have been deemed guilty of constructive treason.

Thus I have seen a copy of a document of the Secret Police in which a pastor is given the option of a fine or imprisonment for an offence against 'the fundamental principles of the National Socialist Movement' on the ground that, as the document says, 'in your sermon at —— on —— 1937, you denied the principle, "If you serve your people, then you are serving God". You said that a man must first serve God; then can he also serve his people.' The demand, 'You shall obey God rather than men' is, it appears, an offence against fundamental Nazi principles. The leaders of the Hitler Youth share the theology of the *Gestapo*, but are more logical about it. In the summer of 1939 boys being trained in the Ordensburg Adolf-Hitler School resolved: 'We, Adolf-Hitler pupils, are pledged only to the Führer, but not to the Jewish-evangelical philosophy or church. We cannot serve two causes (*Weltanschauungen*), the Führer and his greatest enemy. Therefore I . . . hereby announce my resignation from the Evangelical Church.'

Some measure of sympathy is due to the Nazis, who against their will and beyond their comprehension have become involved in very complicated matters of theology. If the sources of creative inspiration are the depths of the German 'soul', and the norm of right is the destiny of the German people as represented and interpreted by the Nazis, no man, or at least no German, could have a conscientious objection to the ordinances and policy of the Party; indeed any failure in enthusiasm must be due to a taint in the blood or some un-Germanic trait in the disposition; conscience demands of Germans that they be devoted to the destiny of Germany; what else could conscience mean? Again, the command to obey God rather than men was admirable and very necessary amongst the mixed populations of the Graeco-Roman world in the first century, but it is meaningless in modern Germany; for the will of God is the destiny of Germany, and there can, therefore, be no obedience to God which is disobedience to the men who declare and realize his will.

It would not be very difficult to retranslate this into terms of the British Empire and our enthusiastic Navy League. We are permitted on occasion to suppose that

> When Britain first, at Heaven's command,
> Arose from out the azure main,
> This was the charter of the land,
> And guardian angels sang this strain—
> 'Rule, Britannia! Britannia rule the waves;
> Britons never, never, never shall be slaves'.

The inspired poet (*vates sacer*) further explains, that, whereas other nations 'not so blest' must fall victim to tyranny, Britannia will remain in freedom and prosperity, 'the dread and envy of them all'. It would seem, indeed, that nothing short of world-dominion is the destiny of the British:

> All thine shall be the subject main,
> And every shore it circles thine.

No man, it is clear, could have a conscientious objection to 'Heaven's command', nor could he serve God by contradicting what the angels sang. It has been alleged that Great Britain's 'secret weapon' against Herr Hitler is a sense of humour. The racial philosophy of Herr Rosenberg is accepted with a deadly seriousness in Germany, but 'Rule Britannia' has not been incorporated into any edition of Hymns Ancient and Modern because we are secretly aware that there is a God in heaven transcendent over men and nations, and an eternal law of justice which has nothing directly to do with the imperial aspirations of Britain.

The Nazi conceives of God as purely immanent in the soul of the German people, of which the Nazi Party is the interpreter and Herr Hitler the embodiment. It is not possible, therefore, in practice to draw any distinction between the will of Herr Hitler and the will of Almighty God. This political absurdity, amounting to blasphemy, arises from the denial of the divine Transcendence. The answer to the Nazi creed is to be found, not in politics, but in theology.

The totalitarian State can find no place for the peculiarities of individual conscience or the divagations of individual genius, for, being itself the manifestation of the divine, its will is the norm of right, its opinion is the norm of truth. The nation is organized on the Leadership principle (*Führer-prinzip*); all departments of the national life must be co-ordinated (*gleichgeschaltet*), each under its appropriate Leader and all subject ultimately to Herr Hitler. The State, therefore, cannot tolerate organized, independent fraternities or fellowships such as scientific, literary or philosophical societies which may be critical of Nazi theories or derive inspiration from foreign and un-Germanic sources. Least of all can national totalitarianism endure the Christian Church which purports to be an international society transcending race and to speak to the nation in the name of a non-Teutonic God. The unity of the nation, the philosophic basis of the State, will be undermined, if Germans presume to study French art or Greek philosophy or Hebrew prophecy. The persecution of science, of religion and of the humanities is not a passing phase in the development of the revolution; it is integral to the National Socialist philosophy.

Private opinions and private ecstasies may be enjoyed by the German citizen provided that they do not enter the sphere of politics. The parsons must merely abstain from politics in the pulpit. But this freedom is less substantial than the words suggest. If we should say in this country that the parsons should stand clear of politics, we should mean that they should not identify themselves with particular political parties, that they should not take sides between one political philosophy and another, and that they should not seek to identify genuine Christianity with any one particular practical solution of a political problem; it would not occur to us to mean that upon great and clear moral issues in the national life the clergy should be bound to silence. But in Nazi Germany the term *Politik* has an immeasurably wider significance than 'politics'. A responsible Nazi official has explained that *Politik* means *totale Deutschheit* or everything that is German. Anything, in fact, is political, if the Government, which means the National Socialist Party, declares it to be so. The demand, therefore, that the parsons and others eschew politics means in effect that they must discuss no matter which the Party does not wish discussed. The Party, for instance, has put in control of the State machinery of the German Protestant Church a number of officials who have no standing in the Church, has given them the control of Church finances, power to dismiss all politically unsatisfactory pastors and to control admissions to the ministry. Any pastor protesting against this high-handed treatment of the Church is guilty of a political offence.

Organized political opposition in Germany has been driven underground; the Universities have been disrupted or silenced; the Christian Church alone has maintained some organized independent life within the Nazi State. Hence the protracted story of Church persecution. But Christians, Jews and Social Democrats are not the only sufferers. The rambling fantasies of Alfred Rosenberg in his *Myth of the Twentieth Century* cover all manner of historical and philosophical fields. To criticize or rebut Herr Rosenberg is an offence against 'the sound feeling of the German people' and therefore against the law. The historians, the philosophers, the men of international sympathies and culture have been silenced, and this not because of the temporary embarrassments of the adminstration but in logical fulfilment of the totalitarian idea.

The totalitarian systems represents an absolutism of the State. This is put very clearly by Benito Mussolini: 'the foundation of Fascism is the conception of the State, its character, its duty and its aim. Fascism conceives of the State as an absolute in comparison with which all individuals or groups are relative, only to be conceived of in their relation to the State.' It is claimed, indeed, that 'a sufficient margin of liberty' is left to the individual, but the limits of this liberty are not set by any rights of conscience or natural law; 'the deciding power in this question cannot be the individual, but the State alone'; the State in this connexion means the dominant political party or the *duce*.

Such regimentation is distasteful to the British, but even for us there would be no escape if we took 'Rule Britannia' quite literally and seriously. The overriding of personal liberty in Soviet Russia springs from a low and unspiritual view of man; the perversion of the idea of justice and the suppression of all intellectual freedom in Italy or Nazi Germany springs from a denial of truth transcending national dreams and of a sense of justice written on all men's hearts. All these political aberrations have their origin in bad theology.

But it is not enough to denounce the Soviets and the totalitarians. They represent protests against the glaring ills of the 'democracies'. Has better theology led us, or might it lead us, to a better social order?

III

PHILOSOPHERS AND THEOLOGIANS

μανία γ' οὐ πασὶν ὁμοία.

COMMUNISM, Fascism and Democracy have a long and often sinister pedigree. There are many admirable histories of political philosophy, and I am not competent to add to them. My thesis is simply that all political questions are at bottom theological or, at least, anthropological, for implicitly or explicitly every political system rests upon some doctrine of man and of the value and meaning of human life.

The theologians, St. Thomas Aquinas, Luther and Calvin have influenced political thought and political history quite as deeply as Hobbes and Rousseau, but it will be convenient to start from the latter as the putative sponsors of totalitarianism and of democracy in the modern world.

I

If Herr Hitler had read Hobbes's *Leviathan*, his often expressed admiration for the British would be more easily intelligible. Hobbes started from a materialistic and despairing view of human nature. Man is a creature at war within himself; instincts, desires and passions are ever at strife for the mastery within him. Man, therefore, must 'pull himself together'; he must achieve some harmony and equilibrium within himself; his inner life is anarchy apart from discipline. But, as all men are by nature at war within themselves, so also are they by nature at war with one another; every man's hand is against his neighbour; even the relation between parents and their children rests rather upon some sort of contract than on nature. Hence the necessity of a completely authoritarian society to make life tolerable on earth.

The argument is simple: anarchy is a state of universal misery; it is man's natural state, but it is in the highest degree inconvenient and undesirable; to escape from it men have voluntarily coalesced into societies subject to law and authoritarian discipline, each man resigning his right of self-defence and self-assertion on the understanding that all his neighbours do the same. Even so, only fear will exact respect for the laws. The sovereign, therefore, whether he be an individual or a group, must stand above the law and enforce it; the State must be supreme over life, property and opinion; no subsidiary associations, social, religious or political can have any rights against the will of the sovereign, and certainly have no right of appeal to any super-national and transcendent law or to any court beyond the confines of the nation, for Right is but another name for the will of the sovereign power. Man is by nature a wild and solitary creature; owing to the disadvantages of this condition he enters into a voluntary contract with his neighbours and constructs the State which is 'an Artificial Man,' like himself free, wild and owing no allegiance to any outside authority in heaven or on earth. This is the philosophy of Leviathan, the totalitarian State. As stated by Hobbes it rests upon the ideas that man is not by nature, but only by contract, a social being, and that man is not a spiritual being made for freedom and for fellowship but a mere engine, for, asks Hobbes, 'what is the heart but a spring; and the nerves but so many strings; and the joints but so many wheels, giving motion to the whole body?' Totalitarianism is a philosophy of despair even when, as in modern Germany, it is tricked out in the habit of romance.

The thesis of Hobbes in the seventeenth century was answered by its antithesis in the eighteenth. Jean-Jacques Rousseau, as Mr. Crossman points out, had much in common with our contemporary D. H. Lawrence; he romanticized the life of the happy savage, idealized primitive emotion, and believing that man is born free and naturally good he was concerned with the cure of the disease called civilization. Optimistic and thoroughly romantic in his conception of human nature he supposed that man has only to throw off the chains of tradition to be once more happy and free and good, for man's misfortunes, as Irving Babbitt put it, are due, not to a fall from God, but to a fall from nature. The human species has been degraded by the institutions of society; the coercive authoritarian State robs him of his true nature wherein he is

> Sceptreless, free, uncircumscrib'd, but man:
> Equal, unclass'd, tribeless, and nationless,
> Exempt from awe, worship, degree, the king
> Over himself; just, gentle, wise: but man.

This is the exact contradiction of Hobbes's view of man's natural wretchedness, but it agrees with his individualism. In both systems man is by nature free and independent of all other human beings, and society rests upon a voluntary social contract. For Rousseau, then, the problem of politics is the attempt to find for his imagined free and delightful beings 'a form of association whereby each uniting with all obeys none but himself and remains as free as he was before'. Rousseau solved the difficulty by identifying the ruler with the ruled. Sovereignty resides, he taught, in the common or general will of the people as a whole; each citizen, therefore, in obeying the State is really serving his own will. This, says Carlyle, is 'a Gospel of Brotherhood, not according to any of the four old Evangelists and calling on men to repent, and amend *each his own* wicked existence, that they might be saved; but a Gospel, rather, as we often hint, according to a new fifth Evangelist Jean-Jacques, calling on men to amend *each the whole world's* wicked existence and be saved by making the Constitution. A thing different and distant *toto coelo*'.

Quaker business meetings proceed only by unanimous agreement; their decisions are truly expressions of the common will of all those present. Such procedure may be called ideal. But, since political assemblies never in fact conform to the pattern of Quaker gatherings, and political necessities will not always wait upon the attainment of unanimity, and, in modern communities, it is impracticable for the whole membership to vote upon all important questions, the sovereignty of the people came to mean in practice the whim of the majority. Thus Hobbes is the philosophic father of the totalitarian State, Rousseau of red revolution. The despair of Hobbes is embodied in the Nihilism of Adolf Hitler; and the naif optimism of Rousseau seems echoed in the closing words of the Communist Manifesto: 'Proletarians have nothing to lose but their chains'.

But in spite of the differences between the two philosophers, who start from antithetic ideas as to the felicity of man in his natural state, the political systems arising from their teaching have many points in common.

First, in both cases law is represented as an expression not of reason but of will. Right in Hobbes's totalitarian State as in Adolf Hitler's is identical with law, and law with the ruler's will; so in Rousseau's dream-land 'the voice of the People is the voice of God'; his successors quickly infer that there is no Right beyond that which the sovereign people has ordained. Neither for Hobbes nor for Rousseau is there above the dictates of the ruler an unwritten, eternal law which is at once universal reason and the will of God. But the heart of man cries out that cruelty and oppression are wrong, eternally and unalterably wrong, whether perpetrated by red cap or by brown shirt. One of the clearest indications of the intimate connexion between theology and politics lies in the discovery that political freedom rests in the end upon the recognition of a law above and beyond the laws of man.

Second, in both these philosophies man is treated as an individual atom. In the Leviathan, ancient or modern, 'the masses' are a congeries of interchangeable individuals who are simply the tools or raw material of the State's activities to be rewarded or 'liquidated' as the authorities may think best. Family life has no ultimate significance or validity: 'at the beginning of 1938 a Catholic mother was deprived of the custody of her own children by the Court of Chancery because she had enrolled them in a Catholic private school, and the official law journal, *German Law* (*Deutsches Recht*), approved of this decision'. Married or unmarried, let women bear children for the State; the Hitler Youth or some equally unattractive nurse will tend their minds and bodies. The negation of all rights of personality rests, paradoxically, upon the individualism which regards each citizen as an atom by himself. Similarly in the Utopia of Rousseau's Social Contract the only bond of society is the advantage or the need of its constituent individuals; self-interest alone holds society together, and there are no closer bonds between men than convenience and contractual obligation. The State, as it has been put, is a kind of Assurance Society for Life and Property; taxes are the premium we pay; the police are a fulfilment of our policy.

Third, Leviathan, the totalitarian State, must dominate and control every aspect of the people's life; it cannot tolerate national—and, still less, international—organizations claiming a relative independence and a binding loyalty. It might have been antecedently expected that a system of government inspired by Rousseau with his romantic fervour for freedom and for individual emotion and his dogma of natural human goodness would have favoured the free development of artistic, literary and religious associations, but the tyranny of 'the general will' works otherwise, and the French Revolution sought, in the name of liberty, to abolish all corporate bodies.

The despair of Hobbes and the romantic optimism of Rousseau result alike in tyranny; their individualism leads directly to its apparent antithesis, the organic idea of the State and of society. It came to be taught that the State itself is more real or ultimate than the members which compose it, that the thinking and willing of the individual is but a temporary and local manifestation of the vaster spirit which is the State, and that citizens are but cells in the more complex body of the community. Hobbes had taught that the State is 'an Artificial Man'; but when it has been claimed that this artificial man has the right to dominate over all the men of flesh and blood that compose it, it is but a step to the conception that the State is the real, and the individual but a transient phenomenon. Professor MacIver, quoting the criticism that 'if, when I think, it is society that thinks in me, there is no thought, and no society', observes further that 'the only centres of activity, of feeling, of function, of purpose which we know are individual selves. The only society which we know is a society in which those selves are bound together, through time and space, by the relations of each to each which they themselves create or inherit. The only experience we know is the experience of individuals, and it is only in the light of their struggles, their interests, their aspirations, their hopes and their fears, that we can assign any function and any goal to society.' In the language of philosophical theology, State or nation or church is not a subsistent metaphysical entity but a relation between persons. In a later chapter I shall not refuse to speak of the State as an ethical organism, but 'organism' here will be a metaphor employed to indicate the close bond between individuals each of whom is a spiritual, ethical, self-subsistent person.

There are many philosophical objections to the theories of Hobbes, of Rousseau and of what Professor MacIver calls the 'organismic' conception of society. I am content to observe that they are all inhuman. Man is by nature neither the cowed wretch of Hobbes's imagination nor the blithe and carefree primitive of Rousseau. We are not mere individuals. Our nature can only find fulfilment in our families and in the fellowship of our neighbours and companions; our home is not a mere convenience, and the organized society in which we find ourselves is not a mere institution demanding our obedience or contractual service, but a spiritual inheritance to which we owe loyalty and love and sacrifice. So also we are not mere 'cells' in the vast organism of the super-personal State but ethical and rational beings for whom the community is both a necessity for physical life and a fulfilment of a natural and spiritual need. Hobbes, Rousseau, and their progeny have led us astray because their doctrines of man are radically false.

II

The names of Hobbes and Rousseau figure much more extensively on the pages of political philosophers than those of Luther and of Calvin. But the influence of the two religious Reformers upon the political life of nations has been immense. Politics and theology are wedded without hope of a divorce.

'Earthly kingdoms', wrote John Henry Newman, 'are founded, not in justice but in injustice. They are created by the sword, by robbery, cruelty, perjury, craft, and fraud. There never was a kingdom except Christ's which was not conceived and born, nurtured and educated in sin. There never was a State but was committed to acts and maxims which it is its crime to maintain and its ruin to abandon. What monarchy is there but began in invasion or usurpation? What revolution has been effected without self-will, violence or hypocrisy? What popular government but is blown about by every wind as if it had no conscience and no responsibilities? What dominion of the few but is selfish and unscrupulous? Where is military strength without the passion for war? Where is trade without the love of filthy lucre, which is the root of all evil?' Newman took a gloomy view of human nature apart from grace. Martin Luther had done the same, and therein became an unsuspecting contributor to the rise of Adolf Hitler.

The typical Lutheran despairs of the world and of 'social progress'; the whole world, as he well knows 'lieth in the Evil One'. In his autobiography, *From U-Boat to Concentration Camp* Dr. Martin Niemöller describes the shock with which as a young submarine commander he found himself under obligation to shoot down a British crew with whom as individuals he had no conceivable quarrel: 'it opened my eyes', he wrote, 'to the utter impossibility of a moral universe'. Christianity, says the Lutheran Professor Sohm, 'begets no Christian ordering of this earthly world'. This preoccupation of Anglo-Saxon Christians with a 'social Gospel' and with political endeavour is the pathetic fruit of fantasy and bad theology: 'It is not the task of Christianity to create a Christian world, for a Christianizing of the world always carries with it a secularizing of Christianity.' Human nature apart from grace is irremediably bad; it is *natura deleta*; it is not fit for freedom; it can only be restrained by force. The task of the State, therefore, is not to set up Paradise on earth, but to prevent earth becoming hell. The State, unlike marriage, is not part of the Creator's original intention for mankind; it is vouchsafed by divine mercy as a result of the Fall and in restraint of sin. Were it not for the coercive power of the State, human life would degenerate into pure anarchy; the State therefore is no more than a surgical bandage to hold together a community which apart from this support would collapse in chaos and utter wretchedness. The basis and *raison d'être* of the State is force. A Christian State is a contradiction in terms as impossible of achievement as a Christian police system or a Christian prison or Christian penal legislation. The State may be better or worse, but, whatever it is, it must be accepted as God's merciful gift in restraint of anarchy and obeyed without any limit except only if it should seek to prevent the preaching of the Gospel. 'Thou art not to revile the civil authorities', said Luther, 'when from time to time thou art oppressed by princes and by tyrants, and when they misuse the power which they have from God.' Obedience is a Christian duty; 'a golden chain is good; it is no worse a chain if some wanton hang it on her neck.' This tradition of passive obedience goes far to explain the else incomprehensible submissiveness of the Germans to their tyrants; and the ruthless and pious Bismarck stands as the classical example of the curious *mésalliance* of power-politics and Christianity.

It is for a theological reason that the political history of Switzerland, Holland, Great Britain and North America has been so different from that of Germany. The French reformer, John Calvin, judged human nature little less gloomily than Luther, but his attitude to the world was positive where Luther's was mainly negative. For Luther the Church of God was the ark tossed upon the waters of a wicked world: if the storms rage, so much the worse; if the sea be calm, so much the better. For Calvin the world was not like the sea but like a salt and treacherous marsh to be reclaimed by the elect. The stern and massive theology of Calvinism has tended to produce men of rugged independence and high moral endeavour. 'Whatsoever things are Scriptural are politic', said one of them; 'what was in the Bible shall yet be in the world.' Society in its fallen state might be a mass of corruption, but it was the task of the Church to establish the divine righteousness on earth. 'We believe', says a modern Calvinist, 'that the divine command to the Christian Church, the command contained in the Scriptures, lays upon her the responsibility for the formation of the State, in so far as the historical situation gives her any power of action at all in this respect. Among the different nations, wherever the Christian Church has any possibility of co-operating with the political life of the country in question, she must use all her influence to get God's sovereign claims recognized, even in the system of legislation, in the administration of justice and in legal decisions.'

England has never quite forgotten 'the rule of the saints' and the Barebones Parliament. The English suppose that the parson's place is the pulpit, and that he is utterly intolerable when he attempts to combine with his own the offices of policeman and of magistrate. The term 'Puritan', therefore, like 'Liberal' in later days, has undeservedly fallen into disrepute. For Milton thus describes the Puritan ideal:

Henceforth I learn that to obey is best,
And love with fear the only God, to walk
As in his presence, ever to observe
His providence, and on him sole depend,
Merciful over all his works, with good
Still overcoming evil, and by small
Accomplishing great things, by things deemed weak
Subverting worldly strong, and worldly wise
By simply meek; that suffering for truth's sake
Is fortitude to highest victory,
And, to the faithful, death the gate of life;
Taught this by his example whom I now
Acknowledge my Redeemer ever blest.

Such was 'the sum of wisdom'.

> Only add
> Deeds to thy knowledge answerable; add faith;
> Add virtue, patience, temperance; add love,
> By name to come called charity, the soul
> Of all the rest.

Such sentiments could have as little have come from Luther as from a disciple of Hobbes or Rousseau; they were exemplified in Lucy Hutchinson's life of her husband, the defender of Nottingham in the Civil War; they went with an inflexible integrity and a strong sense of civic duty. If we are pleased to think of them as typically British, we are justified only so far as Puritanism, resting upon the theology of John Calvin, is a part of our national inheritance.

On certain occasions, as when the Japanese invaded Manchukuo, when the Italians fell upon Abyssinia, or when Hitler marched to Prague, the British people has been filled with a burning moral indignation. This is a genuine emotion, however ill related to our previous policies and however suspect to our neighbours. At such times we are, or we wish to be, a crusading people. At the present time a desire to liberate the oppressed nations on the Continent is as urgent within us as the determination to defend our homes. This deep moral indignation, this sense of a transcendent righteousness outraged, this willingness to pour blood and treasure in a chivalry that seems to others Quixotic is largely our Calvinist inheritance, and it seems very foolish, unless there be a living God.

Not least the political influence of Calvinism, and that mediated especially through the Independents, has been in the preparation for our modern democracy. John Calvin was as little a democrat in the modern sense as Luther, and even the Independents (whose descendants are now called Congregationalists) are not strictly democratic in their Church polity. But one of the potent sources of democracy is to be found in a certain peculiar type of churchmanship.

On 11th November 1620, the Pilgrim Fathers meeting in the cabin of the *Mayflower* and within sight of land, drew up and signed the following document:

> In the Name of God, Amen. We, whose names are underwritten, the loyal subjects of our dread Sovereign Lord King James, by the grace of God, of Great Britain, France, and Ireland, King, Defender of the Faith, &c.
>
> Having undertaken for the glory of God, and advancement of the Christian faith, and honour of our King and country a Voyage to plant the first Colony in the northern parts of Virginia do, by these presents, solemnly and mutually, in the presence of God and one another, covenant and combine ourselves together into a Civil Body Politic for our better ordering and preservation, and furtherance of the ends aforesaid, and by virtue hereof to enact, constitute, and frame such just and equal laws, ordinances, acts, constitutions, offices, from time to time, as shall be thought most meet and convenient for the general good of the Colony, unto which we promise all due submission and obedience.

No study of the history of Parliament or of Convocation will make clear the political principles which the voyaging Fathers had in mind. We must look to the less honoured practices of the Dissenting Meeting House.

These Calvinist lay theologians of the *Mayflower* with their Biblical theology and their high doctrine of the sovereignty of God conceived themselves to be depraved, indeed, in their human nature but saved by grace and chosen by God to glorify his Name and serve his purposes on earth. Their piety was deeply inward and at the same time ethical. Each was accustomed, wrestling in his devotions, to receive, as he supposed, his marching orders directly from his Lord. The appointment of officers in his Church was decided by the solemn vote of the whole assembly; no tyranny of bishop or superior Church court was to be borne; for were not the elect, met in solemn conclave and in the presence of the Lord, able to receive the guidance of which they stood in need? Those who were competent to transact the affairs of the Church must surely be able to compose not less effectively the business of politics, and those who rejected prelacy in the Church were little likely to tolerate tyranny in the State.

Their political institutions, therefore, reflected their Church polity. But it would be misleading to speak of them as democrats. By democracy we mean universal suffrage and occasional plebiscite in the form of General Elections as expressing the sovereignty of the people. The Pilgrim Fathers were concerned with the sovereignty of God, not of the people. The procedure of the Church meeting was transferred to political life as being the appointed means of subjection to the rule of God. In principle the system was theocratic rather than democratic. Second, their form of government whether in Church or State was aristocratic. It was the duty and privilege of the whole body of the community to seek out those endowed with the gifts of wisdom, prudence and organization necessary for the ruler, to appoint them with all solemnity to their office, and having appointed them to obey them 'in the Lord'. The ordinary man had the right to choose his governors and having chosen them the duty to obey them. Calvin is the father of representative government as Rousseau of 'the flapper vote'.

'Democracy' of this Puritan type was essentially the rule of law and not of men. When administered by men of high moral seriousness whose whole concern was to express the will of God in human institutions such a system, if somewhat repressive of the more superficial and expansive elements in human nature, is worthy of awed respect, and it may be that the reputation of Great Britain never stood higher on the Continent than when Oliver Cromwell's foreign policy was rooted in such principles.

But in Puritanism we see rather the idea of a Church-State than a political system. A semi-ecclesiastical experiment of this kind, however exalted, is not to be followed by a mixed society, such as our own, neither pre-eminently virtuous nor supremely base, that is rarely willing to deviate 'from the straight and narrow path between right and wrong'. The rule of the saints may be as desirable as uncomfortable, but it is not 'practical politics' for us nor does it provide a political philosophy. The Puritan's interest, first and last, was ethical. The civil authorities must maintain order and punish vice. Organized society was a necessity and a convenience, not a fulfilment of life, a joy, a spiritual heritage. The State was still conceived as a surgical bandage rather than a living fellowship. Let the wicked be restrained and the virtuous be left alone, without political interference, to promote their ecclesiastic and industrial interests. We are on the way to *laissez faire* and the princes of industrial enterprise.

II

The 'age of faith' faded gradually into the 'Age of Reason', better styled the age of questioning and unbelief. The great schism of Western Christianity in the sixteenth century, which we call the Reformation, left the fundamental presuppositions of men's thoughts unchanged. It marked no such sudden breach with the past as the period called the *Aufklärung* or Illumination, the age of criticism, which we connect with such intellectually corrosive names as Hume, Voltaire and Kant. Luther had spoken of 'the harlot Reason', but the Puritans, as Professor Perry Miller has clearly demonstrated of the great New Englanders, were no anti-rationalists; a strain of humanism irrigated and dulcified their interpretation of the Bible. But the Bible was unquestioned by Romans and Protestants alike. The Age of Reason, on the other hand, was monumentally represented by the colossal statue of Wisdom built by the sculptor Pasquier in the heydey of revolutionary enthusiasm. *C'était la plus triste Sagesse que l'on eut jamais vue.* As the fervours of Puritanism ceased to glow, its forms were secularized; the sovereignty of the people replaced the sovereignty of God, and the Puritan temper, rugged, independent, frugal, stern and venturesome, but now concerned with this world, not the next, remained to force its ruthless triumphs of industrial expansion, and, combining with the cold rationalism of the new all-critical schools of thought, to create the modern secular and capitalistic age from which only now we are, as we hope, emerging through the fires of war.

The asking of questions is the duty and privilege of man; it is the hope and pledge of human progress. The term 'rationalism', then, has two meanings. The political ideas we have so far considered have seemed to spring out of the fervours of the human spirit, penitential, pessimistic, ethical or romantic. Turbulent passions and Titanic energies marked the ages of religious renascence and political revolution. It will be a relief and a refreshment in the next chapter to wander for a while in the quieter pastures of reason and philosophy. Such is the gentle rationalism of the humanities.

But there is another rationalism which we may frankly dub inhuman. It exercises the human prerogative of interrogation in fields where it is not permitted. Not all traditional beliefs are 'open questions' to the inquiring human spirit. Impossible as it may be in science to rule out any question or scepticism as illegitimate, there are certain principles and human assurances which we can only question at peril of our humanity, truths which we can only deny by denying ourselves and our own nature. Philosophy was once the love of Wisdom, and wisdom here was contrasted both with cleverness and information; its concerns were first beginnings and final ends, the value and the meaning of the strange carnival of human life. But philosophy in 'the Age of Reason' (which extends in time to the twentieth century and in geography as far as Cambridge) has become a dissolvent of all principles save the law of contradiction, a virtuoso performance of abstract intellectual acrobatics, an exercise in the ingenuities of scepticism. 'Wisdom', said Dean Swift, 'is a hen whose cackling we must value and consider because it is attended with an egg. But, then, lastly, it is a nut, which, unless you choose with judgement, may cost you a tooth, and pay you with nothing but a worm.'

The assurances and sanctities of home, the conviction that it is right to do right, the claims of patriotism, of justice and of mercy, the sacredness of truth, the infinite significance of beauty and of goodness—about the so-called philosophies that deny the validity of such intuitions and certainties, it is enough to say that they are inhuman. The last argument against the Communism of Rousseau and Karl Marx or the National Socialism of Hobbes or Adolf Hitler is that it does violence to the human spirit, that it denies the principles which, because they are most certain and most deeply bound up with our humanity, should be the starting point of any consideration of the meaning of human life or the due structure of society.

IV

THE VALIDITY OF COMMON SENSE

Τὰ κοινῇ φαινόμενα πιστά.

THE Christian faith is revelation superadded upon common sense. In these chapters we are relatively little concerned with revelation but much with common sense; for what is here conceived as the Christian doctrine of society or the idea of Christendom is but an exalted or quickened expression of that *philosophia perennis* or unchanging philosophy of which Plato, Aristotle and Cicero, as well as St. Thomas Aquinas, are the representatives.

I

But 'common sense' is a term that needs further definition. The current opinions of the majority upon matters where they have no knowledge are of small philosophical importance. But 'common sense', as the term is here used, is more akin to knowledge than opinion. It may be taken to cover those maxims, convictions, and intuitions about life and its meaning which come down to us from the immemorial experience of the race and have been most powerfully expressed by those whose names are honoured in the history of mankind. There are certain views about life which we inevitably regard as symptoms of disease rather than as serious opinions and sober judgements. That it is right to do right, that the performance of justice is an obligation laid upon us, that reverence is owing to wisdom, to innocence, to helplessness, to goodness, that the women and children should be the first, and the captain the last, to leave the sinking ship—these are ethical judgements which, however intimately associated with the Christian valuation of man, are not distinctively Christian but are part of the spiritual inheritance of mankind from the noble and honoured figures of the past.

The political dictators of our time who in conduct and theory have most frankly repudiated the ethical traditions of Western Christendom are themselves unwilling witnesses to this *communis sensus* of humanity, for in their speeches they are quick to exalt the virtues of honour, of justice and of peace, and to repudiate the very notion of aggression. Only so can they hope to appeal to other nations and even pacify the anxious questions of their own. This eager and constant avowal of outmoded 'Christian' principles suggests that these principles are not of themselves the perquisites of any religion but are in some way human and written on the very hearts of men.

Man is by definition a rational creature, because he is by nature endowed with that mysterious faculty of reason which Coleridge has called 'the mother of conscience, of language, of tears, and of smiles—calm and incorruptible legislator of the soul, without whom all its other powers would "meet in mere oppugnancy"'. The unity of humanity rests upon that rational nature which is common to man as such. One of the expressions of Reason is morality.

It has been objected that what is Reason to one is nonsense to another, and that Reason, therefore, is as volatile as quicksilver; it is 'like a dove's neck or a changeable taffata'; in particular, men differ in their ethical judgements. The deviations and divarications of human opinion are, indeed, infinite, and there seems no folly so crass but that some man normally deemed sensible will espouse it as the truth; but human intercourse and 'the ordinary correspondence of life' would be impossible were there not among men a large measure of agreement and a commonly accepted body of truth and experience which is not the less sure because here and there it is disputed by the over-clever or the queer. Burke was of opinion that ultimately 'the standard both of reason and taste is the same in all human creatures'. At any rate the generality of educated men agree on certain principles of truth and falsehood, of right and wrong, of justice and injustice; these principles are sometimes disputed by the clever but never by the simple and sincere.

As we can never demonstrate to the madman that our universe of experience is real and his fantastical, so about these first principles, from which our political thinking should start, there can be no argument; for these ultimate principles are rather judgements of the whole personality than of the logical faculty alone. So Aristotle says that any one who would study ethics or politics should first have been well trained in habits, for in some branches of knowledge the first principles must be learnt by 'habituation'. There is no arguing, and there is no agreeing, with the man who says, 'What other men call evil shall be my good'. Men doubtless differ in their insight as in their bias, but our ultimate convictions about the rightness of right and the goodness of goodness are as objective and certain as any facts in the physical world; they are not matters of optional opinion but of knowledge, or we have no knowledge. When a man gives his life in the deliverance of the oppressed or the vanquishing of an evil, we do not say, 'he may, of course, be a fool'; we know that he is justified. Not all men see the philosophical and theological implications of this assurance, but the assurance itself is the glory of man's nature.

David Livingstone is reported to have said that the commands of the Decalogue—at least in the Second Table—he had nowhere to teach the 'primitive' and unvisited savages of Africa, for these commands they knew already. Our own first forefathers, practising like other savages the ritual of the ordeal, acknowledged therein that, when man's perspicacity failed, there was Some One or Some Thing in the Universe that discerned the truth and would vindicate that justice to which man's heart consents. Amongst the great figures of the spiritual history of mankind—Zoroaster, the Buddha, Confucius, Socrates—there is, beneath all differences of dialect and accent, a singular agreement as to the way in which man should walk, the temper and the character which are becoming.

> The lips of many have spoken words of Life.
> In this, at least, the best agree in one,
> That in well-doing and righteous human life
> Sure pathway lies unto immortal Gods.
> In all the haps and changes of the Time
> And of their World, which those have sought to purge,
> Man's Reason is his lamp and only guide.
> Not uniform is that Reason of a man;
> But warped with every variance of the World,
> His time, place, partiality and his brief years.

The many discordant ethical judgements of mankind do not show the utter relativity of ethics or disprove the common rational nature of all men. The march of civilization is the story of man's progressive apprehension of that which earlier ages saw but dimly and often misconstrued.

The sense of the sacred is an ultimate category in the human soul. It cannot be derived from anything beyond itself. The sacred is that which is of infinite worth or imposes an absolute obligation. Primitive man, of course, does not philosophize about it in that way, but he knows that in the world of his experience there are things and duties more precious than life itself. He may, indeed, project his sense of the sacred upon fetishes, tabus and customs which are unworthy of man's reverence; but, as reason advances, he comes to realize what is the true object of reverence and the true content of duty. The scientist who lives laborious days in the disinterested pursuit of truth, the artist who will starve in a garret if only he may express the beauty he has seen, the martyr who will obey God in the scorn of consequence are all religious men or, at least, are men who illustrate that principle which lies behind religion. Truth, Beauty, Goodness—these are sacred, the object of man's true love and reverence. He, to whom nothing is sacred, all questions are open, and the distinction between right and wrong is blurred, is an enslaved, not an emancipated, spirit.

A civilization may be judged by that in it which is accounted sacred. Where truth and beauty, loyalty and pity are reverenced, where strangers, suppliants and old people, the widow, the fatherless and the stranger are deemed to be peculiarly under the protecting care of God, there we see a flowering of the human spirit and an expression of that Reason which is man's highest endowment. The peril of Europe to-day is not so much political oppression as a degradation of the spirit of humanity. In the Trojan war, when Achilles slew Eëtion, 'he spoiled him not of his armour'; that he could not bring himself to do; his sense of what was fitting held him back; 'but he burned him there as he lay in his rich-wrought armour, and heaped a mound above him. And all around him there grew elm-trees, planted by the Mountain-Spirits, daughters of Aegis-bearing Zeus.' Professor Gilbert Murray cites this passage to show the spiritual achievement of the Greeks. With this high dignity, chivalry and ruth we cannot but contrast the wanton barbarity of totalitarian war and racial fanaticism. That which is humane is also rational.

The great Richard Hooker claimed for the Law of Reason that 'out of those principles, which are in themselves evident, the greatest moral duties we owe towards God or man may without any great difficulty be concluded'; he was nearer to the truth than those unfortunates who through the study of that new science which in Oxford (let the Philistines rejoice!) is called 'Comparative Religion' have suffered a fit of spiritual vertigo and come to see only flux and relativity in ethical principles and spiritual sensibilities. The irrational and the evil mar all human institutions and achievements, but we may not therefore despair of Reason and of those ethical certainties which it is man's privilege to apprehend and his glory to express in personal and social life. Coleridge, more judicious here than Hooker, speaks of 'a deep inward conviction, which is as the moon to us; and like the moon with all its massy shadows and deceptive gleams it yet lights us on our way, poor travellers as we are, and benighted pilgrims. With all its spots and changes and temporary eclipses, with all its vain haloes and bedimming vapours, it yet reflects the light that is to rise on us, which is even now rising, though intercepted from our immediate view by the mountains that enclose and frown over the vale of our mortal life.' The *communis sensus* of mankind, the sacred, the humane and the rational are kindred notions; these are the lamps of civilization; these afford the first principles for politics.

II

In a famous passage of the *Antigone* Sophocles speaks of

> Unwritten laws, eternal in the heavens.
> Not of to-day or yesterday are these,
> But live from everlasting, and from whence
> They sprang, none knoweth.

That which to the Greeks of the classical period was rather a sensitiveness than a theory was taken up into philosophy in later years, and the 'unwritten law' of the Greeks became the 'law of nature' of the Stoics. 'True Law', says Cicero, 'is right Reason, congruent with Nature, universally diffused, constant and eternal, which summons to duty by commanding and restrains from wrong by forbidding. . . . From this Law nothing may be taken away, nor, indeed, can senate or people free us from this Law. . . . But all peoples at every time Law, one, eternal and immutable, shall constrain, and One shall be, as it were, Master and Emperor of all, even God.'

It was a great moment in the history of Europe when the Stoic conception was taken over by the Fathers of the Church, and the 'law of nature' was identified with the moral law of the Ten Commandments. This confluence of Stoic and Christian thought has afforded the ethical basis of our civilization in the West. Thus our British Blackstone, echoing Cicero, wrote in his *Commentaries*: 'this law of nature, being coeval with mankind and dictated by God himself, is of course superior in obligation to any other. It is binding over all the globe in all countries and at all times: no human laws are of any validity, if contrary to this; and such of them as are valid derive all their force and all their authority, mediately or immediately, from this original.'

The Source of our being and the Artificer of our nature is God Himself. That 'law of nature', which, as the Apostle held, is written on the hearts even of the heathen, is an expression of the Reason which of itself is a reflection of the wisdom and 'eternal law' of God. First, then, comes the 'eternal law' of God; second, as reflecting it, the 'law of nature', and, third, the customary and statute law of men, which has no validity except as an approximation to the 'law of nature'. From the Being and Nature of God himself is derived man's innate sense of justice; and justice may be called man's 'natural' law, because, where he commits injustice, he does despite to his human nature, he falls short of the meaning and purpose of humanity. It is the task of human law to give particular and concrete expression to ideal justice; the ultimate sanction of human law is the Wisdom and the Will of God; only as an expression of justice has human law authority. The moral law is in man a reflection of the divine Wisdom or Reason or Word of God; human statute law derives its validity, not from the naked will of the lawgiver, but as an expression of Reason itself. This is the distinction between law as it is the basis of Western civilization and law as it is understood in Nazi Germany.

The 'natural law' then, is an expression of universal Reason. But man is nowhere free from self-deception, and his ideas of justice may be curiously warped in their particular application. John Locke, for instance, says that 'the great and chief end of men's uniting into commonwealths and putting themselves under government is the preservation of their property'. This is reminiscent of an old catechism which to the question, 'What are laws for?' proposed as an answer, 'Laws are to preserve the rich in the possession of their riches and to restrain the vices of the poor.' This gives colour to Marx's view that current ethics are no more than a reflection of the economic order of the period. Traditional morality in Great Britain and America as elsewhere reflects unmistakably the outlook and interests of the propertied class. The Christian Church, too, as a human institution, has often stood rather for political reaction than for social advance and the law of God. But duty is not less duty if it be neglected, and justice is not a chimera though it be denied in practice by those who most loudly sponsor it in principle. 'Shylock's enemy is natural law'; the natural law of justice is not to be identified with 'bourgeois morality'; it is no 'defence mechanism' of the propertied classes or opiate for the proletariat. The heart of man appeals to the eternal law of God against injustice, cruelty, the oppression of the poor and weak; and revolution always claims its right in the sacred name of justice. Never at any time are man's laws fully just and fully rational, but it is as an attempted expression of Justice and of Reason that they have their authority and rightly claim obedience.

That identification of the Stoic 'law of nature' with the moral requirements of the Decalogue was much more than a logical recognition of an historic convergence of ethical ideals, Hebrew and Hellenic. The Stoic tradition was philosophical, the Hebrew was religious. The Stoic conceived morality as an expression of universal Reason; it was apprehended by the Hebrew as the will of the living God. Reason is not enough. It is useless to 'ingeminate peace' or plead for 'sweetness and light', while the barbarian is thundering at the gate. The discovered coincidence of the 'law of nature' and the Decalogue meant that the dictates of universal Reason were vivified and empowered as the expression of omnipotent Will. 'Thus saith the Lord: Go down to the house of the king of Judah, and speak there this word, and say, Hear the word of the Lord, O king of Judah, that sittest upon the throne of David, thou, and thy servants, and thy people that enter in by these gates. Thus saith the Lord: execute ye judgement and righteousness, and deliver the spoiled out of the hand of the oppressor: do no wrong, do no violence to the stranger, the fatherless nor the widow, neither shed innocent blood in this place.' Reason as a flickering immanent principle has become Law as the expression of a transcendent Will. Philosophy has caught fire in religion without ceasing to be philosophy. The noble conduct at which men may aim has become the righteousness that is of the structure of the Universe, and, since Reason is strong as the Will of Almighty God, it is permissible for man

to hope till Hope creates
From its own wreck the thing it contemplates.

The 'law of nature' is operative law. The term 'law' is often used in a metaphorical or special sense by the men of modern science. There is, or there was till recently, a 'law of gravitation'; there is a famous third 'law of thermo-dynamics'; there is an unduly familiar 'law of diminishing returns'. A layman may not presume to determine what 'law' may mean in such a context, but it is distinguished from law in the ordinary sense in that it derives from no stated law-giver and cannot be honoured or dishonoured in the breach. In the Close at Rugby School there is placed a memorial to William Webb Ellis of football fame, 'who with a fine disregard for the rules of the game as played in his time first took the ball in his arms and ran with it'. The 'laws' of football can be broken; the 'laws' of science can, indeed, be disregarded (at the experimenter's risk), but broken they cannot be. We can break our necks, but not the law of gravitation. But the ethical 'law of nature', which we take to be the shadow of 'the law eternal', is law in the strict and proper sense. There is a Law-giver who says, 'Thou shalt', or 'Thou shalt not'; this law may be broken, but, as the case-books of the doctors and the pages of the historians prove, not with impunity. 'And what', said Oliver Cromwell, 'are all our Histories, and other Traditions of Actions in former times, but God manifesting himself, that he hath shaken, and tumbled down and trampled upon, everything that he hath not planted?' The 'eternal law' as expressed in the 'law of nature' is not an ideal; it is not a 'value'; it is not a prejudice or presumption of the elect; it is written upon the common conscience of mankind, and is ineluctable in its effects: 'that which a man soweth, that shall he also reap'.

The State must be founded upon justice, and legislation must be directed by the law of God. By a true instinct, therefore, and not as a 'design to scare fools and credulous people', says Jeremy Taylor, the rulers of antiquity uttered their legislation in the name of God; for, wherever natural justice, honesty and the decencies of life were required, 'these were really the laws of the true God. For the law of nature is nothing but the law of God given to mankind for the conservation of his nature and the promotion of his perfective end: a law of which a man sees a reason and feels a necessity'.

But this 'law of nature' is not, and cannot be, in itself a code. It is no substitute for statute law. The natural law requires that motorists should not drive to the danger of the public, but it cannot prescribe whether the rule of the road be left or right; that is a matter of custom or legislation. No State can be governed by 'natural law' alone. Natural law gives only authority and direction to statute law which, as Professor Brierly says, 'is the conscience of a community expressing itself in rules of conduct appropriate to the conditions in which the members of the community have to live their common life'. But the concept of 'natural law' is vital to the political philosopher as providing both the ethical foundation for the State and an ideal and limit for human legislation.

In the coincidence of Reason and the law of God alone can we alleviate the tension between freedom and obligation, between the demands of intellectual integrity and the duty of obedience. In reaction from the so-called age of Liberalism which demanded unqualified freedom for man as a rational being and decried obedience as bondage to the past, the Nazis have exalted the virtue of obedience to the destruction of all freedom. Each asserts a truth which, being seen out of perspective, becomes a falsehood. 'Man must be free', says Coleridge, 'or to what purpose was he made a spirit of reason, and not a machine of instinct? Man must obey; or wherefore has he a conscience?' A harmony can only be established as obedience is freely offered to a law itself identical with Reason. 'The powers which create this difficulty', he continues, 'contain its solution likewise; for their service is perfect freedom. And whatever law or system of law compels any other service, disennobles our nature, leagues itself with the animal against the godlike, kills in us the very principle of well-doing, and fights against humanity.' The denial of law is anarchy, and the denial of freedom is slavery; but freedom is only compatible with law, when law is recognized as an expression of eternal Justice and universal Reason.

V

A TAG FROM ARISTOTLE

φύσει πολιτικὸν ζῶον.

MANY have taken in hand to tell the story of the origins of human society. There have been very divergent pictures of the 'state of nature' before man collected himself into society. Hobbes, says Professor Babbitt, conceived this as a condition of liberty, equality and war; Rousseau as a condition of liberty, equality and fraternal pity; Locke as a condition of liberty, equality and reason. All these presuppose that society comes into being by some voluntary cohesion of adults. 'We do not by nature seek society for its own sake', wrote Hobbes; 'the original of all great and lasting societies consisted not in the mutual good-will men had towards each other, but in the mutual fear they had of each other.' 'All being born free and equal', said Rousseau, 'part with their liberty only for the sake of their advantage.' So Locke, believing that by nature all men are 'free, equal, and independent', justifies civil government as 'the proper remedy for the inconveniences of the state of nature'. But in truth there never has been since Adam, and never could be, a solitary, independent, self-sufficing human being. Man, says Aristotle, is by nature a social or civic being.

I

Social life is grounded in man's nature, not in his choice or his weakness or his misfortune. Apart from society man would be 'either a beast or a god'. Organized society is not merely a surgical bandage in restraint of chaos, or a convenient mechanism for the supply of physical needs, or an assurance society that one joins voluntarily but with some hesitation as to the value of the policy. The social order has for us a positive value; apart from it we lack something essential to our full humanity, and are not only physical waifs but also spiritual starvelings.

The State, or organized society, exists for the sake of the good life, of human felicity, of the realization of humanity. It was founded, said Aristotle, that men might live, and continued that they might live happily. No man is in fact an independent, isolated, purely individual being, since we can only come into the world as members of some family. The State is, indeed, so fluid a conception that it does not seem to belong to the permanent structure of the world like the family; it is, perhaps, rather an achievement than a datum. But, if to be the father of a family is a good life, to be at once the father of a family and a citizen of a famous State is manifestly a richer and fuller life. The family, therefore, is *societas imperfecta*, a society imperfect because it does not offer full scope to all man's nature. We need the State that we may realize our full potentialities as human beings.

Man is a 'political' or civic as well as a 'social' creature. Opinions differ about the advantages of life in cities, particularly in modern cities. Samuel Johnson said that 'the happiness of London is not to be conceived but by those who have been in it'. There are many who feel like that.

> Piccadilly! Shops, palaces, bustle, and breeze,
> The whirring of wheels, and the murmur of trees;
> By night or by day, whether noisy or stilly,
> Whatever my mood is, I love Piccadilly.

But this is mere gregariousness, and not at all what Aristotle meant. 'I will venture to say', added Johnson, 'there is more learning and science within the circumference of ten miles from where we now sit, than in all the rest of the kingdom.' But even the philosopher's delight in the companionship of letters and of learning still falls short of the Greek conception of man as a 'civic' being. 'Why, my good friend,' says the Athenian stranger to Cleinias in the third book of Plato's *Laws*, 'how can we possibly suppose that those who knew nothing of all the good and evil of cities could have attained their full development, whether of virtue or of vice?' The State is necessary as the school and exercise-ground of character. Man is a gregarious animal and likes to have his boon-companions round about him, but not less necessary to the 'good life' is a society that involves a large circle of unchosen companions, many demands of duty and claims of charity. Man needs the State for the spiritual development of his humanity.

The modern 'liberalistic' individualism derives from a secularizing of the Christian idea of the value of the individual personality. In pre-Christian times for the most part, as in modern Russia and most explicitly in Nazi Germany, the individual may claim no rights against society; the State is conceived as a biological organism like a swarm of bees. These are the two extremes, for in totalitarianism the individual is deemed to have no rights against society, and in individualism to have no duties to it. Both these are false, because one-sided and exaggerated, ideas of man. The Fathers of the Church took over from Aristotle the idea that human nature requires the organization of civil society, but combined with it the Christian idea of personality. From a sociological standpoint Don Luigi Sturzo sees the novelty of the Christian religion in a three-fold contribution to pagan thought. First, by its principle that obedience to God must take precedence of obedience to man it broke down 'all imperative relationship between religion and the family, clan, nation or empire, giving it a personal basis in conscience'. Second, its 'Good News' was universal in its scope, embracing all divisions of society and all varieties of race, and calling all men everywhere to a common life of repentance and of charity. Third, it brought the institution of the Church: 'a single, visible religious society, extraneous to political or domestic institutions, autonomous and independent, founded on definite beliefs reputed as truths, indeed, as truth itself'. It might be objected that Christianity, as the example of Socrates sufficiently shows, did not first reveal to man the existence and obligations of a conscience, and that the Stoics also, with their conception of the 'seedling word' of Reason in every human being and of the *jus gentium*, were international in their thought and doctrine. But, in general, there can be no question that the Christian Church with its insistence upon the responsibility of the individual conscience to the living God and its exhibition of a society transcending all social, national and racial divisions introduced a new element into the problems of political philosophy and radically diminished the old prerogatives of the civil State. Accepting the Aristotelian doctrine that man is by nature a civic being, the Fathers implicitly rejected the 'surgical band' conception of the State; insisting that the individual is of infinite value as a potential child of God, they broke with the 'bee-hive' conception of society. We rightly look back to the great days of Athens as being the fountain-head of democratic life, but Athenian society rested upon slavery. Not till the triumph of the Christian conception of the value of the individual life is the way prepared for a free society of free men.

As a 'civic being' man requires for his normal development a *civitas* or organized society. The phrase 'organized society' is clumsy and unattractive; the Greek term 'city' is misleading and too small; 'nation' or *Volk* is not sufficiently precise, and 'State' has a parchmenty and rigid feel, suggesting not literature but the Circumlocution Office. None the less, 'State' is on the whole our most convenient word, provided it be understood rather in terms of the community than of the law-courts. The family is *societas imperfecta* because it cannot provide scope for the full expression of man's nature. The State, the *civitas*, on the other hand, has been traditionally conceived as *societas perfecta*, because man has no wider needs beyond it. To Aristotle the free and independent city-state was man's blessing, his pride, his world. Outside, beyond the narrow fringe of Greek cities, lay the vast but unnecessary domains of the barbarians. For us, on the other hand, however warm the civic loyalty in our boroughs and municipalities to-day, the single town cannot be the *societas perfecta*; there is the life of our nation, itself comprising three memorable traditions; there is the enrichment that comes from foreign travel and the knowledge of foreign literatures; there is the British Commonwealth of peoples, and there are wider leagues or federations struggling to be born. We must abandon the idea of a limited *societas perfecta* outside which no loyalties are due. The State is not a metaphysical substance, a super-person, but one of many human relationships and associations to all of which in their due place we owe both loyalty and service.

Yet the State has a virtue and authority which it does not share with any other human association. It is distinguished by *suprema potestas*, the right to demand, and not merely to accept, the last sacrifice from its members. For the State is the largest unit of common life and common government in the affairs of this world; it is the association which apart from the Church has the widest and deepest unity; it is the heir and guardian of a tradition that transcends the passing generations and any sectional interest. The State, says Burke, 'ought not to be considered nothing better than a partnership agreement in a trade of pepper or coffee, calico or tobacco, or some other such low concern, to be taken up for a little temporary interest, and to be dissolved by the fancy of the parties. It is to be looked on with other reverence; because it is not a partnership in things subservient only to the gross animal existence of a temporary and perishable nature. It is a partnership in all science; a partnership in all art; a partnership in every virtue, and in all perfection. As the ends of such a partnership cannot be obtained in many generations, it becomes a partnership not only between those who are living, but between those who are living, those who are dead, and those who are to be born. Each contract of each particular State is but a clause in the great primeval contract of eternal society, linking the lower with the higher natures, connecting the visible and invisible world, according to a fixed compact sanctioned by the inviolable oath which holds all physical and all moral natures, each in their appointed place.' So may an Englishman address his fellow-countrymen, and we count that people happy for whom the sphere of sovereign power corresponds with a unity of history and culture. But, as the disunity in many homes does not alter the true meaning of home, so the chaotic and maladjusted sovereignties of many oppressed and unfortunate lands do not alter the true meaning and place of the State in the life of man. The 'nature' of man is that which man is meant to be, and the nature of a political society is that rational and moral end which is a spiritual achievement, not a 'natural fact'. Only as we know what society should be, and may be, can we wisely criticize the present or plan the future.

II

The origin of the State lies in the social or 'civic' nature of man; its end is the achievement of *commune bonum*, the good of the fellowship as a whole. As in a home the particular and individual desires of the members must be subject to the good of the whole family, so in the State the private desires, plans, ambitions and enterprises of the individual citizen must be limited by the welfare of the whole community. This is not quite the same thing as the adage that the State must seek 'the greatest good of the greatest number', for that principle, unless very judiciously interpreted, would neglect or override the interest and proper rights of a minority for the advantage of a mere majority. Rather, it is right that the welfare of all men should be equally considered, and no man should be given privileges to the disadvantage of the community as a whole. The majesty and authority of the State derive from the principle that the State pursues an ethical end; this end justifies the State in its demand for obedience and loyalty and in its exercise of force and discipline. The State thus lies within the realm of ethical purposes; this both affords its authority and limits it. Such a principle is congruous with the contention of the last chapter that the ultimate source of law is God, and that human law has authority only as an expression of eternal justice. The use of force is justified only by the ethical ends which it may serve. A tyranny and a free democracy are distinguished not because, while force rules in the former, it is eliminated from the latter, but because in the former, force serves only the will of the ruler, and in the latter it subtends an ethical end. In both cases the State rests upon force. But the true State is bound together not by force but by loyalty and love and sacrifice.

The common good, to pursue which is the goal of the true State, must not be materialistically conceived, for man is a spiritual being. Food, clothing, shelter and security may be the first necessities for happiness, but a State concerned only with the economic order would very imperfectly serve the common good. Art and letters, religion and the disinterested pursuit of truth are the glory of a community and essential elements in its good life. But these pursuits all presuppose freedom, and, indeed, even an economic order theoretically flawless can bring man no satisfaction, if it destroy his freedom. The State that pursues the common good, therefore, aims at a society of free men and seeks to order and direct the various activities of human life, but to control them only so far as this may be necessary in the common interest. Literature, art, invention, industry are the affair of those engaged in them. The community as such has not the ability to prescribe to artists nor the knowledge to administer mines or cotton mills. The State seeking the common good must keep a paternal eye upon the multifarious vocational and artistic associations in the nation, seeking no more than to provide encouragement, forms and patterns within which the members of the community must themselves achieve the common good, each by following his own vocation in a freedom subject only to the rights and needs of others. Ideally, mining and cotton-spinning and all the other industries should be self-governing corporations subject only to Parliament as representing the whole community. In the present chaotic conditions of our society the nationalizing of great industries may be desirable in the interests of greater justice and greater freedom; this may, perhaps, be a necessary step towards a true social order at once collectivist and free, but in itself bureaucratic control is a limitation of freedom and therefore undesirable. A man may prefer to work for a Government Department rather than for a private employer, for so he may expect juster treatment or more security, but he would far rather work for an industry which he felt in measure to be his own because he had a voice in its management and a personal pride in its production.

The age of individualism and *laissez faire* in politics and of unrestricted competition in industry is gone. In the future we shall have a collectivist society; the only question is whether we shall have a collectivism of tyranny or a collectivism of freedom. The latter is a spiritual achievement. It must rest upon general consent to the principle that the State exists for the sake of the common good and upon a worthy and spiritual interpretation of human nature. Both in theology and politics we fall into grave error if we take an optimistic or a pessimistic view of man. He is a mixed creature, neither wholly good nor wholly bad; as a spiritual being, 'made in the image of God', he has the right to freedom; as a 'fallen creature' he needs the corrective restraint of force. A State that refuses to use force must collapse in anarchy; a State that rules by force and not through the loyalty of free men is on the way to tyranny. The conception of the State as existing to conserve and further the common good is the only way to a society that shall be at once collectivist and free.

The virtue of the State is justice. The State must defend the fundamental human rights of its constituent members, but, beyond that, justice does not involve equality. Justice in politics means that the State both requires and protects the very varied functions of its members; for 'orders and degrees jar not with liberty' (nor with justice) 'but well consist'. God has not made men equal in respect of gifts but only in respect of certain fundamental rights and duties, to which we come in the following chapter. There must be those who labour with their hands and those whose work is clerical; there must be those who give orders and those who obey them;

> For just experience tells, in every soil,
> That those who think must govern those that toil;
> And all that freedom's highest aims can reach,
> Is but to lay proportion'd loads on each.

This no doubt smacks too much of the 'governing class' and the days before universal education, but in substance it is true. Freedom is not incompatible with obedience. It is well that all men should have a share in the government of their country and of their industry; but industry, as little as an army, can be run on Rousseau's principle of identifying the governors with the governed. The Soviet Republics have discovered that by sad experience. Mr. Tom Wintringham's observations about a People's Army are of wider application also: 'it is not the formal framework of democracy that is needed,' he says; 'an army cannot elect its officers and vote on what its tactics and strategy shall be. It is the raw stuff of democracy that is called for: men who feel free, and feel themselves by natural right the equals of their fellows; men who accept regulations and order—restrictions on their individual actions—because they realize the need for these in strengthening their collective actions; men who accept commands as part of inescapable methods by which they themselves can achieve their own desires and aims—an army of free men.' Justice in the State is satisfied as each member is able to serve the whole community in a task and under conditions appropriate to his powers, and receive his fair share of the good life which the society together can attain.

Man belongs to many circles, national and international, cultural and industrial, recreational and religious. The State is one amongst innumerable associations. Its *differentia* is the organization and protection of the common life of a community that shares a common history and culture. The State's authority is derived in the last resort from God, but the mediate source of its authority is the ethical and spiritual end which it properly achieves in the preservation and enlargement of the common good. It is as representing, guarding and developing this common life that the State demands and deserves allegiance, love and sacrifice.

VI

THE ALLEGED RIGHTS OF MAN

Reges in ipsos imperium est Jovis.

εἷς ἐστὶ πᾶσι κοινὸς ἀνθρώποις νόμος.

It is impossible to estimate or imagine the havoc that has been caused in human life by the irreproachable principles of excellent but myopic persons. All heretics and fanatics, however grievously involved in error, have actually seen a truth. 'A mind a little off its balance,' said Oliver Wendell Holmes, 'one which has a slightly squinting brain as its organ, will often prove fertile in suggestions'; yet a virtuous but monogamous loyalty to one principle ('forsaking all other') is the way to disaster alike in theology and political philosophy. Adam Smith, grasping the salutary truth that society derives much advantage from the free enterprise of forceful men, and Karl Marx, discovering the unimagined influence of economic conditions upon human history, have both led humanity, in opposite directions, far astray. Some of our advisers in politics can see only the individual, others only the State, others, again, only the Church. We need a more synoptic or panoptic vision.

But, more deeply, the thought of the modern world has been greatly bedevilled by what Dr. Temple has called 'the Cartesian Faux-pas'. Descartes, he tells us, 'attempted to reach certainty by an all-embracing experiment in doubt'. Upon the proposition, 'I think, therefore I am', which cannot be denied without contradiction, he attempted to ground his philosophy, and from it to prove the reality of God and of the world. He sought, in fact, to prove the reality of the Universe by introspection without reference to the way the natural order and the supernatural order affect us, make their impression upon us and 'environ' us. This method has brought us into a barren desert. It has led to every sort of scepticism. If we will accept for our thinking only that which cannot be denied without contradiction, we shall not go far in piercing the mystery that surrounds our mortal life. 'So far is reality from feeling obliged to meet all our objections', wrote John Oman, 'that it only dimly unveils itself to our most sympathetic and far-reaching insight. This may be highly unphilosophical on the part of environment, yet the fact remains, and even philosophy can only accept it.' In our political philosophy as elsewhere we shall be well advised to start from such first principles, however obscurely they be felt rather than seen, and however difficult at first it may be to harmonize them with each other, which yet represent such deep convictions or intuitions that we cannot deny them without a major operation on our human nature. In other words, we should start from principles the denial of which would involve, not necessarily a contradiction in thought, but a repudiation of our human nature. No battle of words will ever prove, and no balanced judgement will ever deny, that we have a sense of the sanctity of home, of inalienable human rights of man as man, of the claims of our country upon us, even to the sacrifice of life, and, finally, of a duty of loyalty to conscience and to God. These four intuitions need further examination, but we may not ask more of a theory of society than that it is applicable to the world we know, that it is congruous with these deep, if dim, convictions, and that it indicates a way of duty that commends itself to reason and to conscience. In particular, we do well to close our ears to any political theorist, charm he never so wisely, who overrides or ignores any one of these sign-posts or first principles.

The rights of home, the rights of man, the rights of society, the rights of conscience and of God—these we may not claim to demonstrate by logic; but, as man grows in spiritual and intellectual perception, there is a consensus of mankind that there are such rights in nature and in reason. By reason we mean, not logic irrespective of first principles, but those first principles themselves which, because they are our starting points, admit neither of verification nor of argument. The question is not whether the rights of conscience, for instance, can be proved by logic, but whether the man who rejects the *communis sensus* of the nobler of mankind feels himself therein to be a wiser and a better man, and nearer to the hidden secret of man's mysterious life. In our sense of the sacredness of family life, of the obligations of justice, of the claims of others upon us we are given a clue to the great mystery. If we reject it at the instance of some preconceived theory, we may erect a philosophy, but we shall inevitably fall short of wisdom.

I

First, there is no substitute in the life of man for home.

> And, as a hare, whom hounds and horns pursue,
> Pants to the place from whence at first she flew,
> I still had hopes, my long vexations pass'd,
> Here to return—and die at home at last.

It is, indeed, astonishing what unsightly places can be given dignity and beauty by the name of 'home'. In the home we are meant to learn the ways of obedience, responsibility and service to prepare us for life in a wider world. But home is much more than a school of morals or a civic training centre; it is a spiritual unity, rooted in nature, realized in grace; and the mutual relationships of parents and children are rightly regarded as something sacred. 'Let us beware', says Coleridge, 'of that proud philosophy, which affects to inculcate philanthropy while it denounces every home-born feeling by which it is produced and sustained. The paternal and filial duties discipline the heart and prepare it for the love of all mankind.' Plato was for taking the children of his best families out of the constricting circle of the family and educating them in communal fashion. If, he thought, a child did not know his mother from any other woman, he would be the richer by having every woman for his mother. But in this he did violence to human nature. There is no recognized limit to the number of our aunts, but even the most gifted of us can have no more than a single mother.

The family is a social unit, a little, organized fellowship, the foundation of the wider State. But if a man moves his household to the suburbs, plants a hedge round his detached mansion, pays no visits, welcomes no guests, reads no papers, and refuses ever to

> change his comfort and his crony
> For crowd and conversazione,

his life is like that of the poor wretch who blocks the chimney, closes the windows, writes an appropriate letter to the coroner, and turns on the gas. The spiritual claims and 'natural rights' of the family must be related to the claims and rights of communal life. 'The Englishman's home is his castle', but he may not rightly resist the incursion of the tax-collector and, sometimes, the recruiting sergeant. There is tension but not contradiction between the claims of home and of society. The State that will not call its citizens to arms will perish from without; the State that wantonly disturbs the home will be disrupted from within. Happiness, whether individual or social, is always a matter of very delicate equilibrium. The home, then, is a little world, sovereign *in suo ordine*; it is member also of a planetary system of other worlds, and enjoying its own unfettered life it may not wander without disaster to itself and others from its proper orbit.

II

We are vividly conscious of our neighbours' infirmities and our own rights, more particularly when these last are threatened or ignored. Indeed, we are disposed with the anti-Jacobin to condemn the man who will not stand upon his rights as 'sordid, unfeeling, reprobate, degraded'. But when we attempt to define more exactly the alleged 'rights of man', there is a most bewildering variety of proposals, of which Mr. H. G. Wells's recent contribution is the most vertiginous. There has been much confusion between 'natural law' and 'natural rights'. Many, assuming the validity of a 'natural law' of justice in the world, have estimated according to their capacity the forms of a just ordering of society and ascribed the status of 'natural rights' to such arrangements as justice might seem to demand. Thus the right to inherit property or the right to enjoy the fruits of one's labour or the right to say or to drink what one will have all been claimed as 'natural rights', as if they were established, not upon human law but upon human nature. Now, the *lex aeterna* of everlasting righteousness is mirrored in that 'law of nature' which is written upon the consciences of unsophisticated men. But this 'natural law' of justice is no substitute for a legal system; it is indeterminate until it has been expressed according to the needs and conditions of the time in statute or customary law. Thus 'things fair and things just', says Aristotle, 'are liable to such variation and fluctuation that they are believed to exist by law only and not by nature.' But in that case justice on earth, instead of being a manifestation of an eternal principle, will be a mere matter of convention or authority, and the distinction between right and might will be obliterated. The Greeks, therefore, sought to discover man's φύσις, a word we very inadequately render 'nature'; it means the most real thing underlying all manifold changes and appearances. This, said John Burnet, 'explains why the ethical problem, when once it was raised, took the form of a search for φύσις, for an underlying and permanent reality, in the vast mass of traditional morality embodied in the uses and observances which varied so strangely from city to city, to say nothing of the bewildering maze of "barbarian" institutions'. If there are any 'natural rights' of man, they must be inherent in human nature itself and applicable to all humanity,

> While e'en the peasant boasts these rights to scan,
> And learns to venerate himself as man.

The whole idea of 'natural rights' has been brought into disrepute because enthusiasts have claimed that the right to vote or the right to uncensored literary output or the right to bequeath one's property were natural and inalienable prerogatives of human nature. Rights of voting, of printing, of testamentary disposition presuppose Parliaments, printing presses and policemen. We might as well claim that the savage has the natural right to be a man about town as that these doubtful advantages of civilization are our due as men. Most of our alleged human rights are bogus, but, as Fr. L. Watt says, 'to substitute for this belief (that people have rights just because they are human beings) the idea that all their rights are conferred on them by the State to which they happen to belong is to open the door to every kind of enslavement'.

There are human rights only because there are human duties. Man, says the same writer, 'has a natural duty to seek his perfection in accordance with the moral law'. Man has the *duty* to exercise and improve the talents that

God has given him—subject to the moral law that requires him to act justly to his fellow-men. Therefore man has the *right* to exercise his talents. In its most general and abstract form, man's one right is to be a man. What does a man require that he may be enabled to fulfil this duty? It has been generally taught that man must claim the right 'to life, to bodily integrity, to obtain the necessary means of existence; the right to tend towards man's ultimate goal in the path marked out for him by God; the right of association and the right to possess and use property'. Even this list is, perhaps, not wholly beyond the reach of criticism and question. But it will not be disputed that a man has a right to such family life as shall not be inconsistent with the common good, to such education as his intellectual gifts and the possibilitities of society allow, to service of the community according to his capacities, to the worship of God and to obedience to his conscience. None of these rights is demonstrable. It may only be claimed for them that they rest upon an apprehension of man's nature which is congruous with the common reason and conscience of mankind. They can be maintained, though without any secure foundation, by those who would deny that man is by nature a child of God. It is not necessary for a fair degree of human felicity that all citizens be Christians, but there can be no stable and free society except upon an implicit doctrine of man which we derive both from Scripture and from that reason which is man's common and highest gift.

Duties and rights are inseparable, and the latter derive from the former; that is the fundamental principle. The duty of a family is to be a little society of parents and children, mutually dependent and in a special relation to each other, the unit of the wider society. All the rights of the family rest upon this duty. All a man's 'rights' over against the State derive from his duty to give himself in service to his fellow-men; he must be what he can be before he can give what he ought to give. The 'rights' of the State over the individual have as their only and sufficient basis the duty of the State to foster and preserve the common good.

III

Even here we cannot escape altogether from theology. Of all human rights we are apt to put first the right of personal liberty. The institution of slavery man has always resented—for himself; but it was defended by so judicious a philosopher as Aristotle, who held that some men are by nature slaves. Thousands are slaves in all but name in Russia and where the Nazis rule to-day. It is the Christian valuation of man that has made the idea of slavery intolerable, and apart from the Christian faith there is no security for freedom.

But, if the overwhelmingly reasonable Aristotle saw no reason why all men should be free, it might seem that political emancipation is based on revelation, not on reason. It would be wiser to say, however, that there are some truths to which the mind and heart of man, once they see them, must consent. Abstract reasoning could scarcely bring us to the conclusion that man is 'made in the image of God' and as such is of an infinite value; but once the truth is presented to us, we may find it inescapable. This truth may first have been clearly given in Jesus Christ, but even the Greeks were feeling after it—'as certain also of your own poets have said, "for we also are all his offspring".' Reason is not here contrasted with revelation, and, although from a thousand discordant points of view arguments may be adduced against the rights of political liberty, none springs from a philosophy that can satisfy man's deepest intuitive certainties and none can convince the heart.

To return, man's right to political liberty rests upon his corresponding duty to give himself to others in society, and it connotes the obligation to respect the liberties of others. The man who, burdened with 'the weight of chance desires', claims to do whatever he likes whenever he wills is less free than Lord Capel when he wrote in the Tower of London:

> Locks, bars and solitude together met
> Make me no prisoner, but an anchoret.

The liberty of the individual citizen is not incompatible with order and discipline in the State. 'The liberty, the only liberty I mean', said Burke, 'is a liberty connected with order; that not only exists along with order and virtue, but which cannot exist at all without them. It inheres in good and steady government, as in its substance and vital principle.'

IV

Between the highly abstract rights of man as man and the particular rights which in any State may be accorded to the citizens by law there is, I suspect, an intermediate series of rights, hard to define and much neglected by the political philosophers. God made us not only men but members of particular societies. The writer of this book by the grace and predestination of his Creator is an Englishman. Had he been born a member of the French nation, he would have enjoyed certain rights of which now he is deprived. For instance, he cannot say, as any Frenchman may, 'We stormed the Bastille in 1789'. The Englishman, however, has the right to say, 'With the help of God we defeated the Spanish Armada; we produced Shakespeare and Milton, Nelson and Wellington; we gave self-government to South Africa', and the like. A man of prosaic and literalistic mind may protest that these are no more than historical judgements which, if they are true, may be asserted by men of any nationality or none. But, when a schoolboy says, 'we won all our matches this term and got four scholarships at the University', he is asserting neither his personal athletic or intellectual prowess, nor a bare statement about other more gifted persons. *We* won our matches; it was the school, and not merely the team, that won. What British subject does not step the more proudly (and also, we hope, humbly) when he recalls the gallantry of Dunkirk? We have the right to be proud; we are all ennobled by the nobility of others. Though any self-respecting Englishman would die rather than be seen at his prayers or heard talking of the 'English soul', as Germans talk of 'the German soul', yet every Englishman ('else sinning greatly') magnifies in his heart

> This royal throne of kings, this sceptred isle,
> This earth of majesty, this seat of Mars,
> This other Eden, demi-paradise,
> This fortress built by Nature for herself
> Against infection and the hand of war,
> This happy breed of men, this little world,
> This precious stone set in the silver sea,
> Which serves it in the office of a wall,
> Or as a moat defensive to a house,
> Against the envy of less happier lands,
> This blessed plot, this earth, this realm, this England,
> This nurse, this teeming womb of royal kings,
> Feared by their breed and famous by their birth,
> Renowned for their deeds as far from home—
> For Christian service and true chivalry—
> As is the sepulchre in stubborn Jewry
> Of the world's ransom, blessed Mary's Son,
> This land of such dear souls, this dear, dear land.

Walter Bagehot said that 'in real, sound stupidity the English are unrivalled'. This seemed credible till it was discovered in Berlin that Shakespeare was a German! We have, indeed, our grievous infirmities. The English *ne veulent jamais voir les choses, ni comme le bon Dieu les a faites ni comme le diable les a changées.* None the less,

> while yet a nook is left
> Where English minds and manners may be found,

the Englishman is at home and proudly disposes himself to magnify his great inheritance.

Other nations, it may be, have equal privilege but different. An Englishman has the duty and therefore the right, the natural but particular right, to be an Englishman; he has the right to his inheritance. He has the right to a knowledge of English history and English literature, of the English countryside and of the liberties which Englishmen have won. Man has not by nature a right to a Parliamentary vote or to live in a democracy, but those who speak Shakespeare's tongue and hold the faith and morals of Milton 'have titles manifold'. We shall set it down, therefore, as one of the rights of man that he should be entitled to enter into and to carry forward the spiritual inheritance of his country and his people. From such a principle economic and political consequences follow; these may not be neglected by the political philosopher because they differ from place to place and age to age.

Our sense that our country has the right in case of necessity to demand from us the offering of life itself is expressed in the political doctrine of sovereign power. The ground of this right is ethical. It lies in the correlative and logically prior duty of the State to conserve and further the common good. The State has no moral authority apart from its concern for the good of its members as a whole. Apart from justice, said St. Augustine, kingdoms are but bands of brigands. In the common cause the State may demand obedience, but likewise in the common cause the individual citizen may refuse it. Passive, uncritical, unlimited obedience to the State is of no moral worth and is unworthy both of the nature of man and of the nature of the State as a fellowship of rational and moral beings seeking a common end. In the last resort the right of rebellion may be claimed. Because civil war is the most grievous calamity that can fall upon a people, since it means, for the time at least, the end of society itself, any man who loves his country will prevent it at almost any cost. Rebellion in the interests of family or party or class or section is treasonable and rightly treated as a capital crime against society. It was cynically observed by Sir John Harrington:

> Treason doth never prosper—What's the reason?
> If it doth prosper, none dare call it treason.

But rebellion and usurpation are not justified by their success. Violent revolution with the forcible overthrow of the constitution is only justified when government has become intolerably unjust, when the common good is in no sense its aim, and, furthermore, there is reasonable certainty that the misery and chaos caused by revolution will be outweighed by a common good that is attainable and clearly seen. Many revolutions have been attempted in the power of delirious catch-words, such as 'freedom' or 'equality'. But these may give dominance only to greed or to force or to possession. Rebellion can only be justified by that same concrete loyalty to the common good upon which rests the claim of the State to sovereign power.

V

Finally, man has a sense of obligation to his conscience and to God. A classical illustration of this is the famous interview between Andrew Melville and King James in Falkland Palace in 1596. 'Mr. Andro', says the chronicler, 'brak af upon the King in sa zealus, powerfull, and unresistable a manner, that, whowbeit the King used his authoritie in maist crabbit and colerik maner, yit Mr Andro bure him down, and outtered the Commission as from the mightie God, calling the King, but "God's sillie vassall"; and, taking him be the sleive, says this in effect, throw mikle hot reasoning and manie interruptiones: "Sir, we will humblie reverence your Majestie alwayes, namlie in publick, but, sen we have this occasioun to be with your Majestie in privat, and the countrey and Kirk of Chryst is lyk to wrak, for nocht telling yow the treuthe, and giffen of yow a faithfull counsall, we maun discharge our dewtie thairin, or els be trators bathe to Chryst and yow. And theirfor, Sir, as dyvers tymes befor, sa now again I mon tell yow, thair is twa Kings and twa kingdomes in Scotland. Thair is Chryst Jesus the King, and His Kingdome the Kirk, whase subject King James the Saxt is, and of whase kingdome nocht a king nor a lord nor a heid, bot a member. And, Sir, when yie war in your swadling-cloutes, Chryst Jesus rang friely in this land in spyt of all His enemies.'

Our religious liberties were won for us first and foremost by those who were prepared to shed their blood for what they called 'the Crown Rights of the Redeemer'. We know that in the last resort we 'must obey God rather than men'. But the rights of conscience may easily be overstated. An uninstructed conscience is no infallible guide to duty. Before now men have felt impelled by conscience to wear no clothes (wholly contrary to the customs of the period and the requirements of the climate), to refuse to allow their children to be vaccinated, and, most troublesome of all, to refuse to fight for home and country. Must the State permit Doukhobors to travel clotheless to the detriment of their health and the prejudice of public morals; has uncertificated conscience authority to override the Medical Officer of Public Health; how can the State have the moral right to require, and the individual the moral right to refuse, the sacrifice of life in times of national danger? The Doukhobor, it may be, suffers from the conscience that is distempered and oblique, the Quaker from a conscience over-sensitized. Have both an equal right to defy the State? This question has an answer but no solution.

No man may claim the right to an ill-regulated conscience nor to disguise pride, pig-headedness and ignorance under the cloak of moral principle. But an individual's conscience is a matter on which even General Councils, not to mention judicial tribunals, may err. If any man, after searching his heart and taking all available steps to illuminate his mind, is persuaded that he must disobey the State in obedience to God, he has the right, because he has the duty, to follow conscience. The State, on the other side, is bound to foster and, if need be, enforce the common good. The issue may be a deadlock or a tug-of-war. But, since the best wealth of nations consists in citizens of intellectual integrity and moral inflexibility, it is rarely the wisdom or duty of States to interfere with conscience.

But the right to follow conscience constitutes no claim to toleration. The individual has no right to ignorance and moral obliquity. Only to sceptics and perverts are all things tolerable, and even they generally draw the line at conscience.

The State is concerned with human felicity upon this earth; it is not concerned with the last end of man beyond this temporal sphere. That is the affair of the Church. Again, the State can direct, but not create, the virtues upon which its culture and achievement must depend. The direct fostering of virtue is the task of the home and of the Church. The State derives its ethical authority from that total view of man in relation to God of which the guardian is the Church. The State can enforce, but only the Church can inculcate, obedience; and the Church, that it may do this, must be free. The place of the Church in the large economy of life will be the subject of a later chapter.

Meanwhile, on the assumption of the essential soundness of the intuitive convictions of nobler men and of the unity of the human race in ethical reason, I have indicated the place of the State in a hierarchy of ends, set between family, fellowship of humanity and Church, sovereign *in suo ordine* but of no authority beyond, upheld in an equilibrium of tension, a gift of God for the perfecting of human nature, and like all things in the universe exhibiting, according to *analogia entis*, some similitude to its divine Original.

VII

WHEN THE WAR IS OVER

ἐν δὲ δικαιοσύνῃ συλλήβδην πᾶσ' ἀρετή 'στιν.

MAN is by nature a social being; organized society, therefore, is necessary to man's full and happy life; the end and justification of the State is that it should serve the common good. Such principles may offer a standard of criticism of every State but do not of themselves imply any particular organization of political life. Whether monarchy or republicanism, for instance, is better for Eire is a matter that cannot be decided by abstract reasoning or appeals to conscience or to Aristotle. Nor may we expect unanimity of judgement about matters of political expediency. A writer, therefore, is much safer if like the aeronaut above the clouds he be content to breathe the rare atmosphere of abstract philosophy and very general principles, lest descending to earth he be involved in the intricacies, contradictions, contingencies, compromises and relativities of practical politics like poor General Stammfest of Mr. Bernard Shaw's imagining:

'*Stammfest.* "How can I obey six different dictators, and not one gentleman among the lot of them? One of them orders me to make peace with the foreign enemy. Another orders me to offer all the neutral countries forty-eight hours to choose between adopting his views on the single tax and being instantly invaded and annihilated. A third orders me to go to a damned Socialist Conference and explain that Beotia will allow no annexations and no indemnities, and merely wishes to establish the Kingdom of Heaven on Earth throughout the universe."

'*The Grand Duchess*. "Damn their trifling!"

'*Stammfest*. "I thank Your Imperial Highness from the bottom of my heart for that expression. Europe thanks you."'

The appeal to reason and to conscience will be wholly indecisive between different forms of government, democratic, aristocratic, or monarchic, for it is not to be thought that institutions suitable to the tribes of Ashanti will be adapted to the denizens of U.S.A. Any form of government is good and justified as it serve and promote the common good. It is certain that amongst an inexperienced and uneducated people the common good will not best be served by Parliamentary institutions. It is equally certain that to deprive the Briton or American of his share in, and his responsibility for, the government of his country would be retrograde as diminishing the fulness and value of his life.

But the democracies, it is widely said, have failed. New experiments have all been in the direction of totalitarianism and autocracy. Democracy in the West must itself be tested by reason and by conscience. In particular, can it meet and solve the economic complexities of modern life? We are fighting for 'democracy', while all men of sensitive mind must admit that the evils of our democratic system are intolerable. That is our dilemma.

I

The writings of John Ruskin have suffered undeserved neglect. He is wisely forgotten by those who would remain complacent. Then, too, none could read his preface to *Unto This Last* without hoping that his tortured spirit, now released, is observing with a quiet satisfaction how much of his revolutionary doctrine has become the common-place of those who care. Again, the very modern development of Capitalism from competition to monopoly has in some degree put his pleadings and denunciations out of date. How far his diatribes have ameliorated the spiritual and mental state of political economists I cannot judge. These have shifted their ground; some have exchanged Adam Smith for Karl Marx—but without thereby escaping Ruskin's searchlight. The economists still claim that their subject is a happy blend of esoteric mystery and practical science, with which the layman may not safely interfere, and of some of their systems it might still be said that 'the reasoning might be admirable, the conclusions true, and the science deficient only in applicability'.

The science of economics we must leave to the economists, praising their erudition, applauding their prowess, hoping for beneficent and, if possible, consistent wisdom from their researches, and begging them only to remember that the human beings who engage in trade and industry are queer concretions of soul and brawn, reason and passion, greed and loyalty, 'it being the privilege of fishes, as it is of rats and wolves, to live by the laws of demand and supply; but the distinction of humanity, to live by those of right'.

Economists, like theologians and the men of politics, have very often proved unfortunate in their predictions, but to err is human, and we cannot too highly praise and honour those who have 'sought out' economic laws and can understand alike the manipulation of the Bank Rate and the mysteries of the Gold Standard. To these experts we intrust ourselves in times of public sickness with the same anxious mixture of hope and hesitation with which we summon the physician to our private bedside. We come to grief and poverty when we neglect economic laws. Governments are more and more concerned with economic matters, and certain economic theories have even sought to climb into the chair of political philosophy. But in the last resort Great Britain is governed, not by economic laws, but by Acts of Parliament. Economic laws may be as inexorable as the laws of electricity, but we will use both for our own purposes; they must subserve the ends of reason and of conscience; they were made for man, not man for them.

'Man is by nature a social being.' The economic organization of his social life must express and serve his nature. The first and last and always inevitable criticism of the system under which we lived till the outbreak of this present war is that it did despite to human nature both in those who were its beneficiaries and in those who were its victims. We have sought to comfort ourselves with the reflection that 'the lot of the workers has been greatly improved' in recent years. That is doubtless true, but the great disparities in wealth, the hunger and insecurity and unemployment and drab or squalid conditions of a great part of the population have been such that 'the cruelest man living could not sit at his feast, unless he sat blindfold'.

The Socialist, the Fascist, the Communist have their answers ready. But, so far as we have experience of these theories in practice, it does not seem that any one of them by itself is a cure for our distempers. The working classes are probably better off in the democracies than anywhere else in the world, but not the less painful to contemplate or to endure are the evils and the perversions of human nature that seem inherent in our present order.

As in the last chapter I attempted to lay down certain convictions and intuitions of right and duty, which in the end can neither be demonstrated by logicians nor denied by men of good-will, so here I will venture certain criticisms and principles with no further argument than that they make appeal to the reason and conscience of those who view our present social disorder with dismay. They are not, I think, to be denied by any whose consent we greatly value; they offer no prospect of Utopia, but point the way to a possible new world which should make the victims of the present agonies feel that their sacrifices and their sufferings are not in vain.

In the last war, while profiteers from various sections of society were making satisfactory fortunes at home, there was developing in the Army a memorable fellowship of the trenches. After the war the demobilized citizens, who had been assured that their sacrifices were not unappreciated and should be rewarded by a land fit for heroes to live in, found themselves thrown unwanted and unwelcomed upon the labour market, and the gallant officers who raised a few shillings by hawking goods from door to door might be deemed fortunate in comparison with the vast and increasing and hopeless company of the unemployed. To-day, when no man knows whether before sunset or morning a bomb may have dropped upon his house or person, the fellowship of the trenches has been enlarged to the fellowship of the whole nation. Coalescing in a common peril we freely recognize that both our lives and our property must be held at the disposal of our neighbours. It would be intolerable that, when at last the bow is slackened, we should revert to the old order of our pre-war world. By common consent and in recognition of common sacrifices and great experiences gone through together we must order our national life anew. It is idle to make precipitate plans for conditions that we still cannot envisage, but it is none too early to be clear about the principles.

Here we must first seek to be free of the tyranny of names. 'Democracy', 'Capitalism', 'Socialism', are catch-words or 'slogans' of indeterminate meaning with varying associations of terror or delight for different speakers. I have attempted, so far as possible, to avoid them all. If we could forgo the satisfaction of calling one another by opprobrious names we might quickly discover how deep is our agreement.

The crying ills of our time, typified by unemployment, slums and the deliberate destruction of food while men are hungry, should not be ascribed to any peculiar Satanism of modern business men nor to any economic necessity but to a false and inhuman philosophy. It has been presupposed that the State exists, not to serve the common good, but to keep the ring while the strong wrestle for the mastery, or, alternatively, that the common good is best served when all men are kept on the stretch in struggling each for his own advantage. 'Economic liberalism' is the view of those who 'want no interference whatsoever with the individual either from government or from the social pressure of group organizations. They will tolerate no restrictions upon individual initiative or personal enterprise. They are liberal only to the extent that they wish to be liberated from all social responsibility. They call it free enterprise, but the freedom is for those who possess great resources and dominating strength rather than for the weak or those who depend simply on their own labour for their well-being.' Such is the definition given, rather surprisingly, by the hierarchy of the Roman Church in the United States. The Protestant, Professor Reinhold Niebuhr, says more simply, 'Modern Capitalism rests upon the idea that it is not necessary to bring economic activity under either moral or political control.'

In practice this extreme individualism has for many years been greatly modified. Factory Acts, legislation promoting a minimum wage, national insurance schemes, and 'the dole' illustrate the extent of 'State interference' in the interests of 'the workers' and the palliation of appalling social ills. But we still tend to think of such State action as an 'interference' into spheres where, except under abnormal circumstances, the State should do no more than keep the ring. That sheer individualism leads to the anarchy of the jungle and the utter oppression of the unfortunate and weak we recognize. We are held back by the fear that the alternative is the regimentation of the nation by a soulless and unenterprising bureaucracy. Freedom, indeed, is a good no less than order; between the two there may be tension, but in some happy equilibrium the well-being of the State consists. The dismal prospect of an all-comprehensive bureaucracy is mercifully not the only alternative to the chaos and cruelty of individualism or 'economic liberalism'.

We have suffered from a false philosophy of the State. Concurrently our troubles have been enhanced by the gradual concentration of great wealth and economic power in the hands of very few. The great banks and the great combines, 'imparadised in one another's arms' and officially preoccupied less with the Sermon on the Mount than with the fluctuations of the stock market, have become the arbiters of credit and its allotment. Financial magnates are not peculiarly selfish or unscrupulous or unpatriotic; they are victims of the system which permits or compels them to be lords of a power that is vast, because it controls the circulation of money through the body of industry, and irresponsible because they are answerable to none except absentee shareholders voting in subsidiary companies by proxy. The dignitaries of finance have been encouraged to usurp for their own not wholly altruistic purposes that task of national planning which is the duty of the State in the interests of the common good. This is a very grave and far-reaching social ill. Let not the economists tell us it is insurmountable.

The dehumanizing of modern life is expressed and felt most acutely in the operations of joint stock companies limited in respect of liability but not of dividends. The old personal, and sometimes paternal, relations between employer and employed are largely gone. These companies are governed by a Board of directors responsible to the shareholders who look up hungrily for dividends. Their administration is in the hands of a manager who, however gentle and unworldly his natural inclinations, must before all else show substantial profits. The labourers or operatives toil for the profits of the shareholders and their own wages. Industry only incidentally subserves the common good. It seems a horrible, impersonal and unnecessary system. I shall cite an archiepiscopal prescription for the malady on a later page, but here I may intercalate another quotation out of Ruskin:

'Five great intellectual professions, relating to daily necessities of life, have hitherto existed—three exist necessarily, in every civilized nation:

'The Soldier's profession is to *defend* it.
'The Pastor's to *teach* it.
'The Physician's to *keep it in health.*
'The Lawyer's to *enforce justice* in it.
'The Merchant's to *provide* for it.
'And the duty of all these men is, on due occasion, to *die* for it.

'"On due occasion", namely:

'The Soldier, rather than leave his post in battle.
'The Physician, rather than leave his post in plague.
'The Pastor, rather than teach Falsehood.
'The Lawyer, rather than countenance Injustice.
'The Merchant—What is *his* "due occasion" of death?

'It is the main question for the merchant, as for all of us. For, truly, the man who does not know when to die, does not know how to live.

'Observe, the merchant's function (or manufacturer's, for in the broad sense in which it is here used the word must be understood to include both) is to provide for the nation. It is no more his function to get profit for himself out of that provision than it is a clergyman's function to get his stipend. The stipend is a due and necessary adjunct, but not the object of his life, if he be a true clergyman, any more than his fee (or honorarium) is the object of life to a true physician. Neither is his fee the object of life to a true merchant. All three, if true men, have a work to be done irrespective of fee—to be done even at any cost, or for quite the contrary of fee; the pastor's function being to teach, the physician's to heal, and the merchant's, as I have said, to provide. That is to say, he has to understand to their very root the qualities of the thing he deals in, and the means of obtaining or producing it; and he has to apply all his sagacity and energy to the producing or obtaining it in perfect state, and distributing it at the cheapest possible price where most it is needed.'

Apply this to the operations of a Joint Stock Company that has taken the place of the old independent merchant, and it sounds not sentimental so much as idiotic. The first task of a company is to buy in the cheapest market, to sell in the dearest, and, paying Trade Union wages and keeping within the law, to make the greatest profits possible. Companies cannot know 'when to die' but only when to be wound up, and those who serve them can rarely have any other interest than their wages. But observe further that what Ruskin says is not absurd but obviously true of the soldier, the physician and the pastor, and that what he says about the merchant is not in the least absurd in respect of production whether of food or of any other necessaries in time of war. Salaries, profits, wages are not the first interest of men to-day; their first and last concern is national service in the production of the best for the common good. It is no longer true that, in the famous words of Pius XI, 'dead matter leaves the factory ennobled and transformed, where men are corrupted and degraded', for men and women operatives are ennobled by dangers willingly faced and long hours gladly endured, and are transformed by the dignity of working in a common cause. We are enjoying an almost miraculous revolution. Can we keep it when this testing day is past?

II

I cannot guess what indications of mortal malady may be revealed by the stethoscope of the professional economist as he diagnoses the world we have known, but to the lay observer the obvious symptoms of a breakdown of our economic order are these: (1) that in the richest country in the world an enormous percentage of the population never has quite enough to eat and lives in great economic insecurity; (2) that human labour is treated as a commodity to be bought as cheaply and used as far as possible; (3) that industry is organized not for the service of the community but for financial profits, as is seen most clearly in the destruction of food and the limitation of production while thousands go hungry and in need—'so the primary aim of producing food', observes Archbishop Temple, 'turns out to be in practice, not feeding the hungry, but making a profit'; (4) widespread and permanent unemployment of men who could work and produce that of which admittedly the community stands in need; (5) the organization of industry in such forms that the primary concern of one section of the community is the reduction of costs, including wages, in the interests of profits, and the primary concern of a larger section is in the increase of wages for better conditions and more food. We may not like the phrase 'the class war', but at least it is obvious that with those engaged in industry pulling in different directions the nation cannot 'pull together', and that the greatest good of the community as a whole is neither the goal nor the by-product of our industrial organization.

I do not wonder that the victims of this system refer to its beneficiaries as 'parasites' and 'blood-suckers' and in other terms equally disparaging, nor that

> Some gentlemen think it would cure all our cankers
> In the way of finance, ef we jes' hanged the bankers.

But they are inadvertently unfair. Lack of imagination and pernicious myopia are the afflictions of the class that possesses capital, but in war-time 'cook's son, duke's son, son of a belted earl' reveal much the same astonishing and disinterested virtues. The evil lies in the system, not the men. The system is evil because industry is organized for private profit rather than as a public service, and because the conditions under which a large part of the labourers and operatives live does despite to the rights and dignity of human personality.

Charity is no substitute for justice; it has proved a very insufficient corrective of injustice. We have as a people been pre-eminently wealthy and prosperous, and the asperities of our competitive and individualistic system have been reduced by good nature and modified by interference from the State, but

> O God, that bread should be so dear,
> And flesh and blood so cheap!

Any system that puts overwhelming economic power and therewith control over the destinies of millions into the hands of a few unrepresentative persons is fundamentally tyrannical. Is the only alternative the tyranny of Moscow or Berlin? If in the present war we are fighting for freedom, then in the minds of the majority in this country we are fighting against our own past as well as against the enemy.

'It is one of the gravest weaknesses in our national life', says Dr. J. H. Oldham, 'that, in contrast with the totalitarian States, we lack a clear and definite social purpose.' We have thought of the State as a policeman who would appear only when the trouble is over or, at most, when it is getting out of hand. We have not willingly repudiated our responsibilities for our neighbours' needs, but we have failed to recognize that these needs can in the complexities of modern life only be met by political and collective action. Our task is to reconcile the necessity of collective national planning with the claims of freedom.

Our conception of ownership and property is fundamental. There can in this world be no absolute and unqualified possession of material things. 'The earth is the Lord's and the fulness thereof'; we are but stewards of a bounty. Whether the stewardship be exercised through private individuals or the body politic is of secondary importance provided that possession be accounted only stewardship.

Up to a point the possession of private property is a natural right because it corresponds with a natural duty. The nation is a congeries of families, and the family, existing by natural right, presupposes the home, and the home implies the collection of chairs and tables, tea-cups, pictures, ornaments, the cultivation of the back-yard, and all the excitements and intricacies of the weekly budget. Private property as expressed through the free use of a weekly wage is necessary to home life; it is a natural right. But there is the correlative principle, crystal clear in war-time and almost impenetrably obscure in peace-time, that no man has the natural right to the possession or use of private property to the detriment of the common good. The rights of property in general are legal and not moral or natural rights. If in war-time the Government require my bowling-green for a gun emplacement, I may possibly ask for compensation, but I shall not complain of the invasion of my rights. It would seem to follow that in peace-time I may not claim the right to let the charlock and the darnel choke my fields while men go hungry. It is required of us that we much more frankly recognize the claims of society and of the common good upon that which in the past, if we avoided the grosser forms of misdemeanour, we have been allowed to call our own.

We may not cry Socialism and red Chaos when our legal rights are restricted or removed in the interests of the common good. Such self-restraint should be within our reach to-day. To the man who has a comfortable estate and a modest competence from investments, it would surely be intolerable that after the war his companions and deliverers from the Army, the Navy, the Air Force, the Home Guard, the munition factories and those terrifying coal-mines should revert in great numbers to their economic insecurity or slums, while he should continue to disport himself at large in security and ease. The heart, says the prophet Jeremiah, 'is deceitful above all things and desperately wicked', but it would surely recoil from *that*. A closer approximation to justice in our national legislation is bound to cramp the style of those who hitherto have been unjustly favoured. Such a notion is as startling and revolutionary as, on reflection, it is obvious. A 'damned if I see it' attitude is not to be confused with the authentic Nelson touch. Whether after the war the privileged will love justice more than a continuation of injustice is a moral or religious, not an economic, problem.

In respect of these impersonal and therefore unkickable and unconvertible Joint Stock Companies the Archbishop of York has made certain immediately practicable suggestions which he regards as suitable first-steps towards a better order. His proposals appeared in that valuable stimulant, the *Christian News-letter* for August 1940. First he says that 'wherever limitation of liability is granted, it should be accompanied by limitation of profits. Surplus profits should be payable into various funds: (*a*) an equalization fund for the maintenance of wages at a standard rate in bad times; (*b*) a similar equalization fund for profits; (*c*) a sinking fund for the repayment of capital lent or "invested"; (*d*) a fund for the extension of fixed capital; (*e*) a public service fund to be administered as a rule by representatives of the workers (including management) and of the national State or Local Authority.' Second, he urges an application of the Biblical Law of Jubilee; shares, he thinks, should be either 'debentures' and repayable at a certain date or should after fifty years or so lose much of their capital value until with the lapse of time they are gradually extinguished. Third, the contributions of Labour must carry a title to representation on the Board of Directors. Let the experts consider these suggestions in detail—being careful, if they rend them, to offer a preferable alternative. We might hope for general agreement amongst the sensitive that 'something along these lines' is the way of immediate advance.

There can be little dispute that we need a planned national economy, and, if the planning be that of the nation as represented by its government, and if this planning be in the sole interest of the common good of the community, it would seem a matter of secondary importance at first whether the community as such 'owns' all capital or merely directs its use for the common good. But our planned economy must be without sacrifice of our freedom. Escaping from the 'social incoherence' and clumsy cruelty of our past disorder we must avoid the deadly regimentation of the totalitarian systems. The task is urgent. Those who insist upon discussing whether that to which we look is, or is not, properly or partially or technically or hypothetically or upon certain constructions to be called 'Socialism' should be sentenced to uninterrupted residence in our Universities till their deliberations are complete.

It would be unbearable that we should finish the war against the tyrant in Europe only to take up again the class struggle amongst ourselves. The only way by which we may simultaneously avoid the evils of a competitive system and the bondage of a bureaucracy seems to be by the organization of industry in autonomous vocational groups. It is a matter of no importance, except to poets in search of a rhyme, whether we prefer to speak of 'parliaments' for each industry or 'soviets' or 'corporations' or 'guilds'. All those who engage in an industry, whatever their contribution to it, should come to regard themselves as partners in a national service. The duties and privileges, the successes and trials of the business should be the common concern of all.

I suspect that we frighten and mislead ourselves by regarding the legal aspect of 'ownership' as of first importance. That which is part of our life we 'own' in a human, if not a legal, sense. Who owns Shakespeare? Or we might better ask, who does not own him? The real 'owners' of a public park are not the Town Council or the lord of the manor but the citizens and their children who enjoy it. Those who 'own' the village flour-mill might seem to be all those who can call it 'ours' because they work in it or get their bread from it. Our Navy and our heavy industries belong to us all because our lives and happiness depend upon them. In this sense, 'common ownership' is a spiritual fact already; but the phrase 'common ownership', as, for instance, it is used by Sir Richard Acland in his *Unser Kampf*, scares the timid because it conjures up ideas of bureaucracy and expropriation. There is no essential industry in which we are not all concerned, but chiefly and most intimately those whose livelihood depends upon it. There is little to be said for the view that the control of an industry should be wholly in the hands of those who provide its capital, whether these be shareholders or a government department. Humanly speaking, ownership is a matter of degree, and control is another matter altogether.

For the maintenance of our freedom while we abolish the 'class war' three changes are of manifest importance, first that the operatives in any industry should have a due place in its councils; second that 'a living wage' should, subject to the common good, be a first charge on industry; and, third, a recognition that, as Ruskin would put it, a merchant's vocation is not to make profits but to provide.

First, it is reasonable and right that operatives engaged in a business and giving all their service to it should know the affairs of the business and be represented in all matters concerning its management and policy. There could be no objection to this were it not that, as things are to-day, boards of management put first the profits of the shareholders, and there is a tension between the financial interests of the board and the human interests of the workers. Second, while, no doubt, the phrase 'a living wage' is tiresome and inexact, in general we all know what we mean by it, and it is for the experts and economists to work it out for us in detail. A living wage is sufficient to keep a man and his family in reasonable comfort. National or industrial provision for education, for insurance against sickness and for retirement must be considered in ascertaining a 'living wage', but a wage that in any one week just keeps a man and his family from starving and from freezing is not a living wage. The present tendency to maximum profits and minimum wages is inhuman. Third, the task of a vocational group within a community is to meet a public need and fulfil a public service. Subject to the payment of a living wage and a reasonable return on money lent, the function of the industry is to provide the best possible article for the community at the lowest possible cost. Not gain but service must be the motive.

Two years ago such proposals sounded sentimental, revolutionary or fantastic. We are now apprised that they are practicable without violent revolution because in large measure they are already being practised. To-day by universal consent not only life but wealth is held at the disposal of the State. There is strict limitation of private profit. Our munition factories illustrate, not the class war, but the co-operation of management and labour in production for the common safety and the common good; slackness or shoddy is regarded as little less than treason. There is, therefore, nothing impossible or Utopian about these proposals. It is only necessary that we carry over into peace the spirit that now animates us in war and extend in practice the principles that life and wealth are subject to the common good, and that industry is a free co-operative service of the whole community. We are so nearly there in our 'promised land', if only we have the vision and the courage to go forward.

But we know well that, once the common danger is past, the selfish and less reputable elements in human nature will begin powerfully to reassert and insinuate themselves in our thought and conduct. Justice we owe to all men at all times, but we owe more than bare justice to our munition workers and armed forces. But it will be difficult to remember to be grateful. 'We shall not succeed', says Archbishop Temple, 'in subordinating the economic to the truly human unless we subordinate the human to the divine.' There is no separating religion and economics. We must return with new seriousness to the Gospels if we would solve our economic problem.

VIII

A CLEARING IN THE JUNGLE

καλὸν γὰρ τὸ ἆθλον καὶ ἡ ἐλπὶς μεγάλη.

I

IMPERIALISM, *the Highest Stage of Capitalism*, by Lenin, one of the most influential treatises of this generation, has, in Great Britain, at least, been read by comparatively few, but its ideas have insinuated themselves into the minds of many, and have both clarified and befogged their judgement.

The argument, though familiar, may be repeated: In the last forty years or so the present industrial order has completely changed its shape. The free competition of individual firms has given place to the development of immense trusts, cartels and monopolies. 'This transformation of competition into monopoly is one of the most important—if not the most important—phenomena of the newest capitalist economy.'

The result is that 'production becomes social, but its appropriation remains private'. Industry, that is, tends to be as uncompetitive and centralized as it would be under a system of State Socialism, but its profits remain the perquisite of the shareholders. The vast accumulation of power and capital in a few hands is shown by the new role of the banks. These no longer offer a purely technical and auxiliary service to the capitalist concerns: 'there is being developed a personal connexion between the banks and the biggest industrial and commercial enterprises, a fusion of one with another through shareholding, through the appointment of bank-directors to the boards of directors of industrial and commercial enterprises and vice versa'. Business is more and more under the control, and at the mercy, of the banks. There is a further 'personal connexion' between the banks and industrialists on the one side and the Governments on the other.

Next, Lenin points out on the basis of the total securities held in 1910, that Great Britain, France, the United States and Germany between them owned 80 per cent. of the world's finance capital. This indicates another element in the new situation—the export no longer of goods alone but also of capital. This enables the rich to secure a double 'rake-off': they lend the foreigner capital on which he must pay interest and with which he will buy the goods of the creditor, thus further increasing the latter's profits. All this leads to the division of the world among the great capitalist combines. Lenin gives striking examples. Thus in 1907 the German and American electrical interests 'concluded an agreement for partitioning the world. Competition ceased. The General Electric "gets" the United States and Canada; the A.E.G. "gets" Germany, Austria, Russia, Holland, Denmark, Switzerland, Turkey and the Balkans.'

Hence, too, arises the struggle for raw materials and colonies. 'Colonial possession alone gives a complete guarantee of success to the monopolies against all the risks of the struggle against competitors.' A colony is the negation of a 'free market'. The exploitation of colonies with the export of capital brought it about, says Lenin, that in 1915 the income derived by Great Britain from investments 'is *five times* as great as the revenue obtained from the foreign trade of the greatest "trading" country in the world'. Such capitalism is parasitic, and in time the whole country might come to look like some vast and unprofitable suburb where everybody lives on 'unearned income'. Since, however, the equilibrium between the great capitalistic Powers cannot for ever be maintained, this world-exploitation is bound to lead to war.

Such in briefest outline is the argument. It is a careful and disquieting analysis. It has been a truism in the past that Collectivism by eliminating private initiative would destroy efficiency and paralyse industry, and now the pioneers of Big Business have managed to disprove their own argument while augmenting their profits. They have incidentally made easy the transition from 'Capitalism' to State Socialism, should that ever be deemed advisable; for with very little reorganization a board of directors representing the workers and the public interest could replace the board that represents the shareholders. Indeed, at the present time, when governments purchase crops, guarantee sales and effect barter on a gigantic scale, only the experts can decide where Capitalism ends and Socialism begins. In the old days controversy raged between the advocates of individualism like Harold Cox and the sponsors of Socialism like Keir Hardie. To-day the issue has changed. Individualism is dead; some sort of Collectivism there must be. The choice appears to lie between a monopolistic Collectivism of the banks or financial houses and some form of State Collectivism. Reason and conscience must unhesitatingly elect for the latter, provided only that the organization of industry into semi-autonomous vocational groups maintains personal freedom within State collectivism.

Many of the younger generation, having accepted Lenin's diagnosis as a statement of self-evident truth and having no other comparable assurances and certainties in any other sphere of life, were at first much disposed to think that this present war is nothing more than an incident in the inevitable self-destruction of the capitalist order. Many others, less certainly convinced, were harried by the thought that the real issues of the war are not moral but economic, and had the same sneaking sympathy with Germany that they would have with a man who stole a leg of mutton for his hungry family. They feared lest their moral detestation of German methods was being exploited by the astute to win their support for an 'imperialistic' war. This is no longer a live issue. 'Those who say that this is a war between two great Empires, each fighting for the right to rule and exploit other peoples without their consent', says Mr. Tom Wintringham, 'are speaking of a war that is past. They are, to be exact, speaking of Mr. Chamberlain's war. Mr. Chamberlain lost that war. It is over.'

So far as the British Commonwealth is concerned we may claim that at least in principle the day of predatory imperialism is gone. Mr. Wintringham's judgement may, however, be thought to do less than justice to Neville Chamberlain, for it was his Government which even in time of war adopted an entirely new departure in the application of the trustee-principle to colonial peoples. Hitherto we had never gone beyond a contribution to the capital cost of schemes of economic and material development; the whole cost of health services and education had fallen upon the colonies themselves. But early in 1940 the Government asked for the establishment of a Colonial Development Fund, to promote social and educational as well as economic development, endowed for ten years up to an expenditure of £5,000,000 a year with an additional £500,000 annually for research. Not even now may we claim to do all that duty and conscience demand for the backward peoples for whom we have responsibility, but we may justly claim that only in a very limited and blessedly diminishing degree does Lenin's description of imperialism apply to the British Empire.

II

There can be no ideal solution of the tangle of 'foreign politics'. Abstract claims of right and of ideal justice are the fertile source of fanaticism and disaster in practical affairs. We must be content with the possible, the reasonable and the honest. It is idle to raise the question what moral right have the British to 'possess' Malta and Singapore and Gibraltar and the Bermudas and Nigeria and Bechuanaland and various other parts of the earth's surface. We have the legal right to be there, and no question of morals now arises until we are asked what we are doing there. The present distribution of races and dominions over the world is due in very large measure to conquest and in very small measure to 'justice'. History is an irreversible process. It is our duty to redress manifest injustices, but even here there is a natural 'statute of limitations' provided by common sense. We must firmly decline to reconsider the Norman Conquest or to restore Canada and the United States to the Red Indian braves.

But the colonial question is not in principle insoluble. There are wrongs to be put right, but our refusal to return the former German colonies to Herr Hitler was not among them. Lecturing before the outbreak of war Sir Alfred Zimmern said: 'If on prudential grounds we feel that it is necessary—I do not say that it is—to make substantial concessions to Germany under the threat of force, then common decency—not to speak of Christian principle—demands that these sacrifices be made out of our own substance rather than at the expense of our wards. Let us hand over such possessions as the Suez Canal shares or our holding in the Anglo-Iranian oil-fields—interests which involve no human issues—rather than send some of our African fellow-citizens back to pre-Lugardian methods of government. And if it is territory that the Germans must have, well, then let it be our own territory, not that of our wards. I would rather see Eton and Winchester nazified than allow the Nyakyusa to be pressed under the German steam-roller; for Eton and Winchester would emerge, in the poet's words, "bloody but unbowed", whilst Nyakyusa society would be broken beyond repair, like so many other social fabrics, not in Africa alone, that have been disintegrated under the impact of imperialism.'

The British Government has accepted the principle that the Power that 'possesses' colonies must exercise authority in the interests of the natives and with the benevolence of a conscientious trustee. Granted the universal acceptance of this principle a solution of the colonial question is in sight, but, since the undeveloped peoples are themselves defenceless, it is a matter of justice and duty that the nations who sincerely accept this principle should hold and defend their colonies against the world. In July of 1939 a number of Church leaders and students of international affairs met in Switzerland to consider the problems of colonial government and administration. They made the interesting suggestion that a portion of Africa might be set aside for an experiment in the international control of colonies. They laid down nine principles which, in their view, should govern such an experiment:

1. That indigenous peoples must not be treated as pawns of international policy.

2. That the first aim of government must be the moral, social and material welfare of the native populations, and that its goal must be the self-government of the colonial peoples.

3. That the native institutions and, in particular, systems of land tenure, must be used and developed.

4. That missionary work must be freely allowed.

5. That there must be no denial of essential rights on the basis of racial discrimination.

6. That the militarization of the native peoples must be forbidden.

7. That political propaganda in native territories for foreign purposes must be deemed injurious to native society.

8. That subject to the paramount claims of native welfare the principle of economic equality must be encouraged.

9. That such a system must be carried out under the effective supervision of an international body whose members must be independent of national control.

Here, then, is a suggested possible solution of 'the colonial problem' which is said to be one of the chief sources of international enmity in Europe. The signatories make no special claim to novelty in their proposals and freely admit that in part these principles are accepted and acted upon already. Most thoughtful British subjects would admit that in general these principles are just and right, and that, if they could be made the basis of an international control of colonial lands, some such experiment is worthy of all consideration. But this concern for the rights and liberties and welfare of the backward peoples is rooted in the Christian ethic of justice and of the duty to help and protect the weak, upon the Christian valuation of man as of spiritual dignity and worth, as made for freedom, as a potential child of God. These principles have no validity unless the Christian view of man be true. Neither Nazi Germany nor Communist Russia could possibly accept them. The colonial question is, no doubt, economic and political, but it is at bottom theological or religious. Those who ascribe the present war to Capitalism or Imperialism have a measure of truth upon their side, but, more deeply, this is a war of religions, and there is no possible solution of the problems of the war that is not ultimately theological. Without a common ethic and a common doctrine of man there can be no world-society of nations.

III

The cartels and combinations of modern industrial capitalism have an international outlook; every soap king in his own locality aspires to a world-wide empire; nations, however, are regarded not as historical and spiritual achievements but as markets. Communists would replace the imperialism of finance with the internationalism of the proletariat. But both Marx and Lenin curiously overlooked or under-estimated the explosive force of national feeling. What Stalin thinks no man can tell, but he acts like a Russian patriot delivered from the scruples of bourgeois morality.

National feeling is an excitement with a rational basis. There have been deep schisms in the body politic of Great Britain; but we know and understand one another and sharply distinguish ourselves from 'foreigners'. Our sense of national unity rests upon the unique architecture and climate of the islands we inhabit, upon the common speech which we misuse, upon common traditions and customs, a common and glorious history. A tolerant and condescending people, we are prepared to believe that other nations, less gifted no doubt and enjoying a respectable, though less impressive, history, may after their fashion feel for their nation much as we do for ours. Human life is enriched by these varieties of national culture which are not transferable and are lost in composition. In Europe, in spite of intense difficulty and confusion in Polish corridors, Transylvanian mountains and borderland countries generally there are certain clear national groups which are natural or historical unities. The national State corresponds to a spiritual reality.

For Aristotle the single Greek city with its eager and

multi-coloured life was in itself *societas perfecta*, sufficient for the fulfilment and expression of all man's natural powers; in later ages the *regnum* or separate State seemed to be spiritually self-sufficient. To-day, as we have seen, a wider knowledge of other lands and cultures, a vivid sense of our economic interdependence, the development of new ways of transport and communication, the emergence of new groups such as the British Commonwealth of nations make it obvious that even the nation is not *societas perfecta*. That social life may be 'perfect' or even tolerable, some international order must be established.

Our present state is anarchy; a drab and uniform cosmopolitanism, unattractive in itself, would destroy the values and realities of national life. How, then, shall we conceive an harmonious order among the nations of the world? If we were to consult the theologians, they would offer three principles for our consideration.

First, St. Augustine says, in *The City of God*, that 'the peace of men is an ordered concord. . . . The peace of all things is a tranquillity of order. Order is a disposition of things like and unlike that ascribes to each its place.' St. Thomas Aquinas, with a fore-looking eye, it might seem, to our recent unquiet years, says that we must not identify peace with mere concord, for a concord that rests upon fear or coercion is not truly peace: 'peace is the tranquillity of order'. It must rest on justice.

Second, they would say that the universe is a system set to mirror 'the manifold wisdom of God'. In human life the unit is the person, an individual, subsistent, rational being. But man for his true good needs ampler relations —family, nation, the wider fellowship of nations. As the family is a little order in which parents and children have different duties and responsibilities, so the nation is a larger order in which governors and governed, statesmen and farmers, doctors and craftsmen have their different functions and obligations. So humanity, too, is, or ought to be, an order in which each nation must play its appointed part. The universe, because it is a universe, represents, as St. Thomas says, 'a certain harmony, that is, a proportionated concord'. The universe is an hierarchical system; international relations cannot be the one surd in it.

Third, they would say that the Being of God is the efficient, exemplary and final cause of the order in the universe, that every beauty in the world shadows and in its fashion represents the divine Beauty which is its great Original; we seek, therefore, an order among the nations which, freely accepted, shall glorify God as do the stars in their appointed courses. This, they add for our encouragement, is not just a beautiful ideal, a dream. However difficult of attainment, it is immanent in the structure of the world of man; it is the appointed goal which sin may thwart but can never make unreasonable or intrinsically unattainable. International relations, like all other relations in the world, are to imitate or represent or shadow forth some aspect of God's Beauty and God's Wisdom. That at which we must aim is that to which the whole universe is pointing.

The philosopher starts from the manifold and complex data of the senses and comes, or hopes to come, at the end of his reasonings to unity and simplicity and God. The theologian moves in the opposite direction; he starts from God and descends to see all the manifold of the universe in God. In these days when we are like to be overwhelmed with the complexities and entanglements and confusion of international politics, it is refreshing and hope-restoring to consider the testimony of the theologian, because, while he offers no immediate solution of our difficulties, he suggests that we have all the moving forces of the universe on our side when we work for international order. *Vindex est enim orbis justorum*—'the world fighteth for the righteous'. (Wisd. xvi. 17). It would seem that, if there be a God, what the theologian says accords with reason.

IV

Peace and a stable international order can only rest on justice. But what is justice in this sphere? There are two types of justice, which we may call equal and unequal or 'distributive' justice. The former requires an 'equality of quantity', the rendering of an equivalent; it corresponds with arithmetical proportion. Unequal or distributive justice, on the other hand, requires an 'equality of proportion'; it is, in particular, the justice of the State in ascribing privilege or duty; it corresponds with geometrical proportion. It is just that schoolboys of equal age and equal needs should have an equal amount of pocket-money; that is a matter of equal justice. But after a football match it is just that the team should have a larger tea than the rest, because their service to the community gives them greater need; that is distributive or unequal justice. Is, then, the relationship of nations to one another to be governed by equal or by unequal justice?

The claim that all nations, large and small, have equal or identical rights, as, for instance, that each shall have one vote, and one vote only, at an Assembly of the League of Nations, presupposes equal justice. But when ratios are discussed in disarmament conversations, it is never suggested that no nation should have a larger navy than any other; it is assumed that 'distributive' or unequal justice should be the rule. There is manifestly some confusion here. Are we to contemplate a society of nations each treating every other as an equal with identical rights and duties, or do we look to a society of unequals, for each of which justice depends upon its freedom to fulfil its peculiar responsibilities and duties? It seems an obvious fact in nature, and therefore in God's purposes, that the nations are unequal in respect of opportunity and duty. All nations like all men may have certain fundamental and inalienable rights, such as the right to exist and make their contribution to the whole, but that does not make them equal. The Chinese nation and the Italian, for instance, may be equally meritorious, but they are different and unequal physically, mentally and culturally, as their lands are different and unequal; they have different contributions to make to mankind's common life. If it be just to render to every man according to his need, we must aim at unequal justice in international affairs.

Justice can only be met by a supernational authority. Even if every nation upon earth were a radiant centre of 'sweetness and light', there would still be need for a planned international economy and for the ordered co-operation such as is evidenced in the non-controversial activities of the League of Nations. At the present stage of the world's history order must be enforced. Every society presupposes an authority, and a society of nations is no exception. This supernational authority, as the learned and careful authors of *A Code of International Ethics* are not afraid to say, 'will have power to govern with full sovereignty, to direct the collaboration of nations to the higher good of human community, to summon to its supreme tribunal the disputes which may arise between nations, and to use necessary constraint against any State which would dare to disturb order and international peace'. No State, they add, 'can be allowed, under pretext of safeguarding its independence, to forswear all allegiance to international society'.

How Utopian this sounds! We shall not hope to set up such an international authority when this war is over; it is entirely beyond our present horizon, for the national philosophies adopted by Germany, Japan, Italy and other nations are inconsistent with its fundamental basis. But it is something that we know where we would go, and it is not beyond the bounds of hope and practical effort that

China, the United States and the British commonwealth of nations with such other likeminded friends as they can gather might make an impressive clearance in the present jungle, and, as other nations come gradually to a better mind, enlarge its well-defended frontiers.

V

This does not mean that national sovereignty must be repudiated but only that it must be more carefully defined. The demand for unconditional sovereignty, sometimes sheltering under the claims of self-determination, is one of the obvious causes of our international chaos. In itself the demand for national sovereignty is legitimate and necessary. Only when it is isolated and exaggerated does it become a danger.

In God's world there can be no absolute sovereignty over either people or things for men or nations. *Regem habemus*—only God is sovereign. All human authority derives from him and is therefore subject to his moral law. The national State is truly and rightly sovereign *in suo ordine*, but its sphere is limited. It is limited by the universal moral law. As the State has not unqualified authority over the family or the individual, so also it is not without obligation to all other States. National sovereignty to-day is normally interpreted to mean that each State is at liberty to regulate its own affairs without any outside interference and without reference to any principle but self-interest. Morality, it is said, does not apply as between sovereign peoples, and there are no supernational rights. This is moral anarchy, and it leads, as we know, to political anarchy as well. It is contrary to reason, for we dwell in a universe in which each part is related to the whole, and all is subject to the providence and direction of a common Author.

The collapse of the League of Nations was largely due

to the unconscionable claims of 'national sovereignty', a doctrine regarded as sacrosanct by the politicians of all nations except the predatory. In reaction it is now widely claimed that national sovereignty must be abandoned in the interests of some United States of Europe or Parliament of Man. But the doctrine of national sovereignty is true and necessary provided it be correctly stated. Sovereignty is not primarily an independence of other States but an inherent quality of the State itself. The idea that sovereign States exist side by side without moral relationships to each other is like the depressing and mistaken picture of primitive man in his natural state as depicted by the philosopher Hobbes. We may admit the moral anarchy which obtains between the nations to-day. But this is a breach in nature, not an expression of man's true nature or φύσις. The different countries of the world are at this moment inextricably bound together by mutual needs both physical and spiritual. The sovereignty of the State is *potestas suprema* only *in suo ordine*. The self-sufficiency of the State to organize its own inner communal life is not inconsistent with the rights of the community of nations. A league of nations, so to put it, exists already in reason and in natural right.

The State has its true sovereignty within the realm of ethical ends. The divine law, said Heraclitus, is the source of all human law; the State, neither usurping the place of the family nor isolating itself from humanity as a whole, takes its place in the universal Providence of God as the guardian and dispenser of the common good for each of the various peoples of the world. Thus the sovereignty of the State is limited by the law of justice, by the rights of the family and of conscience, and by the claims of the whole human family. In the sphere of humanity there is not yet an order but only the urgent need for one. It is antecedently probable that, when an international order is established, individual States will properly hand over some of the tasks which have been duties during the period of chaos, and that, as the immediate good of the family must on occasion give way to the good of the whole society, so the immediate good of individual States may under certain circumstances have to give way to the good of the whole family of nations.

VI

What limitation of present rights, then, is compatible with the full exercise of that sovereignty which every State may claim? Can a State, for instance, be expected to renounce the right in the last extremity to levy war? This is usually held to be the ineradicable prerogative of all free States. It is logically derived from the primary right to existence. If a State has the right to exist, it has the right to defend its existence against all challenge. The Duchy of Luxembourg, we conclude, has the right to arm itself against both Germany and France. A small State, in fact, has the right to be destroyed with fighting or without fighting, as it thinks best! Such a right can hardly be regarded as very precious. The analogy of the smaller society would suggest another conclusion. The individual citizen has the right to claim that the State maintain order and preserve him in the enjoyment of his liberties. The analogy suggests that the individual State has the right to demand of the international authority that it be defended in its existence and its liberties, and that its right or duty to levy war at its own discretion is limited to the period of international anarchy. When a police force is available, private vindication of justice is curtailed. In happier days, when France stood erect by our side, *The Times* of the 3rd November 1939 indicated that the appointment of a Supreme Council and an inter-Allied High Command involved 'a standing organ or government with a powerful influence over two distinct sovereign States and a combination of armed forces under unified control'. A moral collapse rather than military disaster brought that hopeful experiment to an end, but since then the British commonwealth and the United States have committed themselves clearly but undefinedly to a joint defence of the American continent without any suggestion that the lawful claims of national sovereignty have been infringed. There is in principle no reason why a Supreme Council and a common High Command representing many States should not in peace-time as in war-time be fully consistent with the inalienable rights of States participant.

Again, can a State be expected without despite to its proper sovereignty to renounce the right to such markets and trading as it can secure? 'We are very well aware', wrote *The Times* of the 19th November 1939, 'that our prosperity is inseparably linked with the prosperity of all our neighbours. It is of the very essence of British economic doctrine that trade rivalry between nations is natural and healthy; we have always sought to develop it into trade co-operation.' *The Times*, it would seem, was for once a little flustered. We have always regarded trade rivalry as healthy, it says, and have always tried to develop it into its opposite! It is self-evident that trade rivalry, where advantage must be to the strong or the fortunate, cannot lead naturally to international justice. A fortnight earlier *The Times* had pointed out that 'steel, tin, zinc, aluminium, rubber, sugar, tea, meat, and other vital products are already under some form of international control'. It seems clear that, when the war is over, the distribution of food and necessities to starving and impoverished countries will be under the control of more fortunate governments acting together; but a planned international economy will be permanently necessary to the world's well-being. It is obvious that, if an international organization could guarantee to Great Britain her just and fair share of the world's butter, bacon and bread, no rights of national sovereignty could justify a claim to more.

But all proposals for international control of armaments or distribution are utterly chimerical in a world of National Socialism, of *sacro egoismo*, of Germany's new order in Europe or Japan's in Asia. International control is only possible on the basis of common ideals and common moral principles. The League of Nations collapsed because it presupposed in its members ideas of justice and of duty and of desire which in fact they did not share. But a Common Council and Zollverein between the British Empire, the United States and China, because we share common ideals, is practicable now. Many would add Russia. In theory this would be impossible, for the Communist Party does not share with these others their ideals of freedom and of justice; of Russia, therefore, it would be wisest to say 'Not yet'. The security and economic advantages of membership in a fellowship of such like-minded peoples would be so great that other nations, who at heart are with us, would quickly join and should be admitted whenever they could give practical evidence that their motives were sincere. We must have a supernational authority, and the reasonable way towards it is by a relatively modest beginning amongst likeminded States and empires.

VII

The State in theory coalesces with the nation, and the unity of the nation rests upon common speech, common traditions, a common culture, common ideals and a common history. But the richness and value of a culture depends largely upon the variety from which it is composed. The Nazis would eliminate from the body politic all non-Aryans and confine citizenship to pure-blooded Germans only. This type of inbreeding is disastrous. The national unity of Great Britain is not qualified but enriched by the divergent traditions and gifts of English, Scots and Welsh; we have been further enriched by Huguenots and Jews and Flemish and Germans who have made their homes amongst us. The United States offers the most conspicuous example of national unity resting upon diversity of inheritance and race. Political boundaries in Europe cannot coincide with racial distinctions, and the problem of minorities remains insoluble, so long as minorities are regarded as troublesome and unwelcome aliens by the majority and are themselves withholding from the country of their dwelling the gifts which they inherit. 'If we take the establishment of liberty for the realization of moral duties to be the end and object of civil society', wrote Lord Acton, 'we must conclude that those States are substantially the most perfect which, like the British and Austrian Empires, include various distinct nationalities without oppressing them. Those States in which *no* mixture of races has occurred are *imperfect*. A State which is incompetent to *satisfy* different races *condemns* itself. A State which labours to *neutralize*, to *absorb*, or *excel* them *destroys* its own vitality. A State which does not include them is destitute of the chief basis of self-government. The theory of nationality, pure and simple, is a retrograde step in history.'

A consideration of international politics most signally illustrates the main thesis of these pages that theology and politics are inextricably bound together. Both the abstract reason of the theologian and the concrete perplexities of the statesman require an international order which in itself implies an international authority. Apart from these, world-peace and justice are impossible. Yet there can be no such international authority except upon a common basis of ideals of freedom and of justice. The British commonwealth, the United States and China (with Russia on the fringe) could make a clearance in the jungle, pool their economic resources to their immeasurable advantage, and organize a common defence against the barbarian till he mended his manners and his principles. International politics are no field for sentiment nor for despair.

IX

AN ETHICAL DILEMMA

ἐν τῇ αἰσθήσει ἡ κρίσις

LAW and order must be enforced, or the world will fall apart in chaos. But what has the enforcement of law and order to do with the Sermon on the Mount, with the highest morality, with forgiveness unto seventy times seven, with non-resistance to evil, with the attempt to imitate God who sends his sun and rain impartially on thankful and thankless, on just and unjust alike? The attempt to enforce law and order may involve the world in war, and war seems to necessitate a moratorium on rational ethics, not to mention the commands of Christ. The elusive but highly moral 'man in the street' is disposed to say that the Christian pacifist is right but futile, that here at least the teaching of Christ appears a brave dream, a fair ideal, but of little practical significance except to enhance our disgust at the iniquity and waste of war. The case has been succinctly put by Hosea Biglow:

> Ez fer war, I call it murder,—
>   There you hev it plain an' flat;
> I don't want to go no furder
>   Than my Testyment fer that;
> God hez sed so plump an' fairly,
>   It's ez long ez it is broad,
> An' you've gut to git up airly
>   Ef you want to take in God.

We might quote Sancho Panza in support of the view that pacifism, quite apart from the commandments of the

Bible, is the way of common sense: 'Sir, I am a peaceable, tame, quiet man, and can forgive any injury whatsoever; for I have a wife and children to maintain and bring up; so that give me leave to tell your worship by way of hint, since it is not for me to command, that I will upon no account draw my sword either against peasant or against knight; and that from this time forward, in the presence of God, I forgive all injuries any one has done, or shall do, me, or that any person is now doing, or may hereafter do, me, whether he be high or low, rich or poor, gentle or simple, without excepting any state or condition whatever.' War is folly and iniquity; *stulte suscipitur*, says Erasmus, *impie geritur*, *misere finitur*—it is conceived in folly, it is waged with impiety, it ends in misery. War is, indeed, folly and iniquity; yet it is the general sense of mankind that on occasion to renounce the way of war is also wickedness and folly. The 'pacifist' issue is not a controversy between the sensible and cranks; it is every thoughtful man's dilemma.

I

Does the highest morality or the Christian ethic involve pacifism? From the sub-apostolic age till the time of the Emperor Constantine it was widely felt in the Christian Church, and emphatically taught by many in authority, that the bearing of arms was incompatible with the Christian profession. From the time of Constantine till 1914, apart from the Society of Friends and certain smaller sects, it was generally taught and agreed that in a 'just' war a Christian might actively participate. After 1918 there was a great revulsion of feeling and much searching of heart in this matter. 'Pacifist' impulses were fortified by a lively sense of the horrors of war under modern conditions, of the futility of war as evidenced in the political chaos of the times, and of the immense difficulties in defining a 'just' war. If military service was not expressly condemned in the New Testament, yet, it was argued, war is utterly incompatible with the Christian spirit, it is 'the denial of the way of Christ' and 'treason to the Kingdom of God'. From 1918 for fifteen years the 'pacifists' appeared to have the better of the argument, and, where they failed to convince, they stirred the conscience of the Church. The plain man said that the Church was hedging on the matter.

Many 'pacifist' arguments, however, presupposed a community of nations open to reasonable persuasion, to moral considerations and to the mollifying influences of good-will. But Herr Hitler's seizure of power in 1933 changed the whole situation. The British people could no longer appeal to the German people; Herr Hitler closed all channels of communication, repudiated as softness and *Humanitätsduselei* the pacific ethics of the Western world, and, pretending might as the source and arbiter of right, presented neighbouring countries with the alternatives of submission or of war. Even so the traditional 'pacifist' argument would not have been overthrown had submission meant merely some loss of political sovereignty and some modification of political freedom. But National Socialism aims at a domination over the minds and souls of men (and, more particularly, of children) as well as over their fortunes and political life. It soon became clear, too, that Herr Hitler's demands for a colonial empire would mean for primitive peoples not a mere substitution of one European domination for another but a régime of openly admitted repression and exploitation in exchange for a suzerainty that, in spite of many blemishes, acknowledged and aimed at the duties and responsibilities of trusteeship. The ethical question, therefore, for the British, was no longer whether the loss of political freedom and the dominance of Fascist policy was preferable to the disasters and iniquities of war, but whether war was not a lesser evil than the spiritual devastation and degradation of the Nazi philosophy and the handing over of the helpless colonial peoples to robbery, exploitation and the reversal of all the aims and principles alike of British policy and missionary endeavour. It is not surprising, therefore, that of those who saw the issues few maintained their 'pacifism'.

Even so, however, the 'pacifist' case was not fully met. War is an acknowledged iniquity. Can it ever be right to do wrong? War violates the first principle of Kantian ethics, that men must be treated as ends not means; it contradicts very plainly the spirit of the Gospel. Is the moral question solved by the claim that war was unavoidable?

> So spake the fiend, and with necessity,
> The tyrant's plea, excused his devilish deeds.

Civilization connotes the enforcement of law and order; war is involved in its preservation and maintenance at the present time. If the 'pacifist' rightly interprets 'the mind of Christ', then, there can be no such thing as a Christian civilization, and the idea of the State sketched or suggested in previous chapters may be 'reasonable' but can make no claim to the name of Christian. Nor is this only a problem for the professing Christian. Conscience and compromise seem mutually exclusive terms. Does not conscience require all men to live up to the highest principles they see, and what is the use of ideals that are not practicable?

For all, therefore, except those who have adopted Communist or Nazi morality (which is not really morality at all) it is a vital question whether the teaching of Christ involves the 'pacifist' position. Here argument by the bandying of texts is unsatisfactory and inconclusive, but *prima facie*, if we look to spirit, intention and logical implication, the 'pacifist's' interpretation is strong, if not overwhelming. It is well that we should consider its full force.

The 'pacifist' admits that the commands, 'Thou shalt not kill' and 'Resist not evil', do not directly refer to the question of military service, and that we must be guided rather by the spirit than the letter of these sayings; but concerning the spirit of such passages, he says, there is no doubt. 'It was said to them of old time, Thou shalt not kill. . . . But I say unto you that whoever is angry. . . . It hath been said, An eye for an eye, and a tooth for a tooth, but I say unto you that ye resist not evil. . . . I say unto you, Love your enemies, bless them that curse you, do good to them that hate you, and pray for them which despitefully use you and persecute you, that ye may be children of your Father which is in heaven, for he maketh his sun to rise on the evil and on the good, and sendeth rain on the just and on the unjust' (Matt. v. 38 f., 44 f.). Granted that the 'letter' of the texts here is not strictly relevant to modern war, can there be any reasonable doubt about the spirit? 'If in our Lord's view the right spirit issues in a "letter" of this kind', asks Dr. C. J. Cadoux, 'how can a "letter" of a diametrically opposite kind be consonant with the same spirit?'

The 'pacifist' argues, further, that our Lord was put to death on a political charge as 'the King of the Jews', that claiming to be Messiah he deliberately refused to lead a political insurrection against the Romans, that he even declined to take any steps to deliver St. John the Baptist from prison, and that the narrative of the Temptation at the beginning of his ministry finds its chief significance in his refusal to achieve spiritual ends by earthly means and win dominion over the earth by taking the way of Satan. This same dominant principle, it is urged, is revealed supremely on the Cross where we see God's way of redemption and of victory over the hearts of men in sharpest contradiction of man's way of force and war. The New Testament, it is true, says little directly about war, but it makes very plain that the sole motive of the

Christian as of his Master must be redemptive love; such a motive seems for ever incompatible with a bayonet charge or a bombing expedition.

Again, the purpose and the work of Christ was the ingathering of the Christian Church as a company of people committed without qualification to the way of Christ, his very Body and the instrument of his will and work on earth, a fellowship transcending all earthly barriers of race or nation or class or sex: 'for as many of you as have been baptized into Christ have put on Christ. There is neither Jew nor Greek, there is neither bond nor free, there is neither male nor female: for ye are all one in Christ Jesus' (Gal. iii. 27 f.). The Christian Church is the new Israel, a brotherhood closer than any ties of race, recognizing no allegiance except to Christ, and dedicated to the redemption of mankind. Such a supernational society committed to live by the principles of the heavenly Kingdom can have no part nor lot in the devilry of war.

Like ourselves the Jewish contemporaries of Christ very sharply distinguished between this present world and the ideal world which they called the Kingdom of God. But nothing is more distinctive of the teaching of Christ than his insistence that with his own coming the powers and the reality of the ideal world were already impinging upon the present world. The precepts of the Sermon on the Mount, accordingly, were not mere ideals practicable only in a better world whence sin and evil had been abolished, but were the principles of the new Kingdom by which 'the sons of the Kingdom' were to be guided even now, since for them the Kingdom had come already. The 'pacifist' is right in claiming that the obedience demanded by Christ is absolute; there is no suggestion that thought of consequences or considerations of local circumstances or pleas of necessity could excuse the disciple from living by the principles of the heavenly Kingdom. To follow Christ is not merely to deny self but also to deny the world with its false judgements, its half-lights and its unspiritual methods. It would appear to follow, therefore, that no plea of intolerable wrong or of political necessity can justify the Christian in abandoning the way of love and taking up the sword.

II

The 'pacifist's' case, so far as it goes, has been made out. Attempts to justify belligerency by the Sermon on the Mount are futile. For himself Christ repudiated the way of violence and was concerned with redemption only. The Christian is called to live without hesitation and without compromise by the principles of God's Kingdom. This is not to be denied. The answer to the 'pacifist', if it be an answer, lies in the indication of other principles, no less integral to the New Testament and to the idea of Christianity, which find no place in the 'pacifist' interpretation.

'Who made me a judge and a divider amongst you?' said our Lord. He had been called to intervene in a dispute between two brothers as to the just division of their inheritance. He declined to enter into the question; instead he bade them both 'beware of covetousness'. He was concerned with the springs of life from which just or unjust conduct arises, with the redemption of the sinner. But may we safely conclude that, being concerned with redemption, he was wholly unconcerned with justice? Refusing for himself the office of a judge, did he mean to imply that no follower of his could be a judge, or that the fair division of earthly goods was a matter in which his disciples might have no interest? Did he repudiate human justice and that which the political State must represent? Was he a 'spiritual anarchist'? Professor Quick tells of 'an Indian Christian who, being heavily in debt and having unexpectedly received a large legacy, distributed the whole sum to the poor of the neighbourhood, paying nothing to his wealthy creditors and keeping nothing for himself'. He comments that this Indian Christian 'overlooked the fact that Christian charity and generosity begin where legal obligation ends, but not before'.

Our Lord accepted the civil and ecclesiastical organization of society in his world—not without criticism and grief, but without denunciation. The law of mercy and of justice as laid down in Deuteronomy and in the prophets he received as the will of God; by bidding men render his dues to Caesar he clearly recognized Caesar as having some place in the divine economy. Even if his attitude to Rome was one of acceptance rather than approval, he clearly regarded the civil-religious constitution of Israel on the basis of the Old Testament as resting upon the will and good pleasure of God—though in the new Kingdom the Law was to be transcended. His demand of a righteousness 'greater than the righteousness of the scribes and Pharisees' should not be interpreted as a disparagement of law and order or as the requirement that his disciples should disinterest themselves from the tasks of the society in which they lived.

The teaching of Christ presupposes the background of human civilization. Where the Church does not find civilization, it must create it. Thus, if Christian missionaries go to a savage country, they first tell the story of Christ and preach the Gospel; but, having won an acceptance of the Gospel, their task is not yet finished; they must provide the braves with some occupation as a charitable alternative to head-hunting; hence they organize agriculture and encourage peaceful trade; schools must be set up; civilized conceptions and practices of justice must take the place of the savage trial by witch-doctor or ordeal. In other words, the Church creates a civilization as a necessary consequence of its evangelistic mission. But every civilization is by its very nature sub-Christian in the sense that the justice of the courts is always different from the mercy of the gospel. Since, then, it is not to be thought that true disciples of Christ must not participate in the upholding of the civilization which the Church presupposes, or necessarily creates, we must hesitate to interpret the absolute demands of the Sermon on the Mount as incompatible with the support of civil society.

But can the Church which sponsors an alternative to head-hunting in Samoa condone war in Europe? War is not civilization but, rather, its denial. Admittedly we cannot conceive Jesus Christ wielding a bayonet on the battle-field; but may we deduce from this with certainty that under all circumstances the use of the bayonet is forbidden to his disciples? We cannot conceive Jesus Christ as accepting the duties of a policeman or butcher or as sitting upon the bench to administer man-made law or holding office as a hangman or a Foreign Secretary in a semi-Christian Government; but we may not securely infer from this that no true Christian may perform these diverse functions. Canon Barry raises the pertinent question whether there can be such a thing as a 'Christian' action: 'is it not rather that there are Christians acting, with greater or less fidelity to Christ's spirit, on the raw material which life gives them, in the job that has to be done where they are?' The argument that our Lord would not use a bayonet is, therefore, not really decisive by itself. Christians believe that he was the Saviour of the world; that He came to manifest the divine mercy of God, to bring the Kingdom of heaven to men, to die for the sins of the world. To have assumed the office of a policeman, a butcher, a judge, a hangman or a statesman would have been inconsistent with his mission, impossible for him but perhaps required of some of those who follow him. No man could share in his vocation to be the Saviour of the world; here he stands alone. Those who would be his disciples must follow him in many different vocations—as husbands, parents, citizens. The obedience Christians owe him knows no limits, but they cannot directly argue from what became him to what is required of them. Our Lord contemplated not the abolition of the Law but its fulfilment in the perfect law of love; it might therefore be inferred that, until the law is transcended, it must be enforced, and that its temporary enforcement is as intimately the concern of Christians as its ultimate transcending.

It is alleged that a certain martial bishop in the Middle Ages was accused of swearing on the field of battle. 'Sir,' he replied, 'I swore in my capacity as officer, not as bishop.' 'But, when the devil has the officer', came the answer, 'what becomes of the bishop?' The Christian is called to live both by absolute ethical principles and as a citizen of the earthly State which itself also exists by the will, and in the Providence, of God. He lives, as it were, in a transition period and belongs to two disharmonious worlds, to both of which his service and his loyalty are due. He owes "a double but not a divided allegiance". In more theological terms his dilemma has been clearly put by Fr. Alec Vidler: 'On the one hand, order has still to be preserved and imposed by force. Its necessities have still to be complied with, else history would lapse into self-destruction. . . . On the other hand, into the order of nature and law another order has broken, the order of super-nature and divine grace. The Christian has to live in both orders, as a citizen of the earthly city, state, or commonwealth to which he belongs by nature, and as a citizen of God's eternal kingdom to which he belongs by grace. The former has to be governed by a legal system which makes use of coercive sanctions, and which, though it can always be brought into closer conformity with an ideal natural and moral law, can never achieve more than an approximate distribution of justice. The kingdom of God is a realm of pure love; in it there is no compulsion but the inner compulsion of love.'

Between the 'Everlasting Yea' and the 'Everlasting

Nay' there can be no compromise, and to do right is always right. But under many circumstances it may be right to do that which in itself is far from the ideal. In popular speech we divide acts into right and wrong, good and bad. To give to the poor, we say, is right and good, to kill a man is wrong and bad. But common sense supported by the Charity Organization Societies has taught us that there are circumstances when indiscriminate giving to the poor is neither right nor good. So it is wrong and bad to kill a man except on the happily rare occasions when it is right and necessary. Strictly, actions (not classes of act) are right or wrong, motives are good or bad. If classes of act could be satisfactorily catalogued as 'good' and 'bad', 'right' and 'wrong', we could get up our duty as a sergeant absorbs the King's regulations, and all our problems of conscience could be solved by a text-book with a reliable index. Actually our moral problem is an often delicate and doubtful decision between various courses of possible action, none of which may be ideal, but one of which is presumably best and therefore right, for it must always be right to follow that which under the circumstances is the best course possible. The moral enthusiast who says that *under no circumstances* will he perform some act such as the killing of a man is refusing to face the real problem of morality. We contrast the conduct of the Good Samaritan in the parable with the behaviour of the bandits and of the priest and Levite. The Good Samaritan did right; the others, we agree, did wrong, but we may not universalize this judgement, and argue that it is always wrong either to use violence or to 'pass by on the other side'; for, had the Good Samaritan appeared on the scene when the bandits were at work, he would have been compelled to take one course or the other; he must either have resisted the bandits or played the Levite's part. One or other of these courses, therefore, would have been right. The 'pacifist' is disposed to argue that our Lord in virtue of the majesty of his presence and the purity and charity of his heart would have caused the bandits to cease their violence without having recourse to violence himself. That we may not dispute. But it is an alternative not open to us except in so far as we are like him.

There are many occasions when the ideal is obvious and impracticable. It is very certain, for instance, that war is not the ideal and Christian way of dealing with Adolf Hitler and his gang. We contrast the way of war with the ideal and Christian way of Foreign Missions. But, so far as the victims of Nazi tyranny are concerned, our choice is not between the wicked way of violence and the Christian way of missions, but between the way of violence and the way of 'passing by on the other side'. This is the typical news brought me by the post on the morning when I was making a first draft of this chapter: 'the invasion of Denmark by the Nazis has brought about 6,000 Jews under the oppressive rule of the Nazis, among them a number of Jewish refugees from Germany who have thus again fallen under the terror. . . . In Poland the persecution rages as severely as ever. In Lodz, where the persecution is particularly severe, a pogrom took place in the Jewish ghetto on March 8. Fifty Jews are said to have been killed, a number of them after being tortured by the Nazis. Over two hundred were wounded. Every Thursday between 30 and 40 Jews are executed by the Gestapo and new arrests are made. Ghettos have now been established also in Cracow, as the *Krakaue Zeitung* writes, "for sanitary reasons". . . . The bread ration for Jews has been further reduced. The death-rate of the Jews in Warsaw is enormous. About 200 die daily; ten times the pre-war death-rate. The number of mental cases increases rapidly, the asylums are full.' Jews, Christians, Social Democrats, liberals of every kind are suffering like this wherever the Third Reich extends its power or influence. They have no hope of deliverance in this world if we refuse to succour them. No means is open to us but war. War is an unspeakable evil, but passivity may well seem a greater evil. To spare the Germans is to refuse to help the impotent and needy; it is to keep our own hands 'clean' at cost of the degradation of men, women and children in soul and body. Most Christians will therefore judge that this is a case where the way of the sword is right.

It is objected that we may not 'do evil that good may come'. The objection rests upon the view that acts in themselves and apart from circumstances are good or evil. We may never do wrong that right may come. But if under the tragic circumstances of the hour war is, of all possible lines of action, the best, then it is also right.

It is objected, further, that, as figs will not grow from thistles, so peace and reconciliation cannot come from war. That is very true. War can destroy, it cannot build; but, if it be judged that there can be no rebuilding of Europe till the Nazi oppression be swept away, then war is creating the conditions without which there can be neither peace nor reconciliation.

The present situation has made many of the arguments of the 'pacifist' irrelevant, but it has not destroyed his case. If any man should say that, much as he sympathizes with the logic and the spirit of those who with a clear conscience go to war, yet for himself the vows of loyalty he has taken to his Master seem to him to preclude his personal participation in the fighting, there can be no argument or moral disapprobation; a man must be loyal to his conscience; that is his first duty to God and to society. If any man, realizing in any degree the issues of the hour, judges that submission is morally preferable to violent resistance, argument will be in vain. But the judgement of most men of moral seriousness will be against him, and he may not safely claim that the New Testament is on his side.

X

THE SECULAR STATE

Nunquam libertas gratior exstat
quam sub rege pio.

I

When the new constitution of Eire was promulgated, it was found that the document began with a solemn acknowledgement of the Blessed Trinity. This was generally regarded by the British as another touching Irish whimsicality. The British themselves are, of course, in a confused and slightly self-conscious way a Christian nation; in the south the society called the Church of England is part of the national constitution, and in Scotland there is a national Church so subtly designed that the lawyers themselves do not know whether it is, or is not, 'established'. On the other hand, the British Empire boasts its neutrality in matters of religion, and it is a question whether His Majesty is *Fidei Defensor* in his Moslem empire. Even in Great Britain the King, himself being a member in good standing of two churches which are not in communion with one another, takes no cognizance of the theological tenets of his subjects. All this is generally regarded by other peoples as symptomatic of the stupidity or the perfidy of Albion. In the United States of America, sometimes known and praised as under the special favour of heaven, the total and irremediable divorce between the State and the Church is deemed one of the bulwarks of liberty. In Germany Adolf Hitler, who declares 'we would have no other God but Germany', has based his constitution upon Christianity of the 'positive' variety. But, in general, those nations that boast their liberal modernity assume that the modern State should be tolerant of all theological opinions and should defend to the last its ecclesiastical neutrality. It would seem obvious that Parliaments elected upon the modern generous franchise are not competent to decide between the competitive claims of sects and scepticisms. On the other hand, one might suppose that the Being of God and his moral law, if such exist, cannot safely be matters of public unconcern. Even the dictators cannot wholly escape the insistent question of the right relations of Church and State.

This question has a long and varied history. The Christian Church began as a small, illicit and often persecuted sect. Remembering the command to 'render unto Caesar the things that are Caesar's', it was in general ready to recognize 'the powers that be' as ordained of God and worthy of obedience, but under persecuting emperors such as Nero, Caligula and Domitian the Church was apt to see the secular power as Antichrist. But through the early centuries the Christians, debarred from any active part in politics, tended to be negative in their attitude towards 'the world'. With the conversion of the emperor Constantine, with the recognition of Christianity as the official State religion, and, a little later, with the vast tasks imposed by the irruption of the barbarians into the empire, a positive and constructive attitude to politics was forced upon the Church. There gradually arose the medieval system which was Christian in so far as it was dominated, inspired and to some extent controlled by the Christian Church; it was in large measure an ecclesiastical civilization. The schism of the Reformation finally disrupted the medieval synthesis, and the astounding doctrine of *cujus regio, ejus religio* became a principle of statesmanship. A more irreligious principle it would be difficult to conceive, for no one (unless it be the King's grace) can change his theological principles with his domicile. With the Reformation, therefore, came the national churches. Parliament and the Prince usurped the functions of the papacy; organized religion—to its great peril —was subject to the State. Such was Queen Elizabeth's Settlement, of which Bishop Hensley Henson says that 'it belongs to a Past which can never return: it has little hold on the Present, and less hope for the Future. Its passing away, which cannot be long postponed, may conceivably release spiritual energies which it can now only hamper and conceal.' With the Age of Reason came the secular State, dedicated to illimitable tolerance and to the complete separation of the State from ecclesiastical entanglements. The last phase is the Communist or other totalitarian construction where the State itself becomes the source, the instrument and the object of a secular religion.

None of these mutual accommodations of religion and the State is fully satisfactory. It cannot be well for the State that the Christians should abstain from any active part in politics. On the other hand, clerical domination of the State, like lay intervention in theology, leads to many disastrous inconveniences. State control of religion, likewise, is as futile as State control of letters, and there is nothing to be said for settling religious truth by reference to a postal address. More recent experiments are not more promising; a State boastfully indifferent to God is not likely to prosper if there be a God, and the secular religions are recognizable as idolatry.

Happily, however, before the close of the medieval period a more satisfactory solution had been adumbrated by Christian philosophers: the State being properly sovereign and autonomous *in suo ordine*, it was not for the Church to usurp the functions of the civil power; on the other hand, the State must recognize the Church in its own sphere as another *societas perfecta* with the proper concerns of which the civil power may not interfere; no doubt, there are common spheres of interest where a mutual understanding must be reached, but in principle the spheres of Church and State are different. This seems in theory a reasonable answer.

II

It implies, however, that the State cannot be neutral in religion. Our present British civilization, as Mr. T. S. Eliot has pointed out, is neither Christian nor pagan, but neutral—with a traditional Christian bias. This cannot be a stable or permanent condition. Some general philosophy of life, Christian, pagan or materialist, must underlie public education and the political, industrial and cultural order. A society that lacks a cohesive philosophy and regards all questions as open is on the way to dissolution. Because toleration is prized amongst us, and clerical interference in politics and education has been the cause of division and bitterness, we are reluctant to recognize that the State at peril of its coherence cannot be neutral in religion and 'philosophy'. This does not mean that an already overburdened Parliament is called to decide between the nice distinctions of metaphysical schools or rival Christian denominations, but rather that there can be no national unity nor lasting social fellowship except upon the basis of commonly accepted principles about the obligations of justice, the purpose of society and the meaning of human life.

Those who do not themselves go to church but desire a free and humane civilization for their country could not be indifferent if the Church of England were to assume Nazi principles or go over to the tenets of materialism. They would probably admit that their own ideals of freedom and humanity would have small 'survival value' were there not a Church to bring the sanctions and reinforcements of religion to the support of the ideals of reason. The State cannot be neutral in regard to the Christian religion, because it must itself rest upon a philosophy of life which is both humane and 'Christian'. 'Grace presupposes nature', say the wiser theologians. The State as such is not concerned with 'grace', 'the supernatural' and the distinctive dogmas of the Christian profession, but reason and conscience of themselves point to that interpretation of life of which the Church's faith, as Christians suppose, is the culmination and fulfilment. A Christian society is not the same thing as a society consisting solely of devout and instructed Christians; rather it is a society resting upon commonly accepted principles which are at once the 'natural theology' of the Church and the dictates of reason and of conscience.

The State must have its own 'philosophy', but even so it needs the Church; for the various 'orders' of Creation —family, State and Church—each independent in its own sphere are in other matters dependent on one another. First, there can be no lasting felicity for a human society apart from the fear of God, which is the beginning of all wisdom. The worship of God is a function which the State can neither neglect nor perform on its own account. The sacring of the King must take place in Church. Second, while the State uses force in the maintenance of justice, it lives by the virtues of loyalty, sacrifice and love which find their meaning and sanction in that spiritual world of which the Church is minister. The State can teach virtue, but the Church imparts it. Again, the State is concerned with human life only upon this planet, but the human beings for whom it legislates are, as many beside the Christians have supposed, also spiritual beings with a destiny beyond 'the flaming frontiers' of this transient world. The State, therefore, in its concern for the good life for man must foster religion, as well as music and the arts, as necessary to man's true happiness. Finally, the State is concerned with justice; beyond that it cannot go. But justice is remorseless and very terrible. Because 'there is a sore wound at the heart of humanity', there is great need of a physician. This the State can never be; it is the office of the Church. The State is concerned with justice and the external act, the Church with redemption and the internal motive. The judge upon the bench may administer with humanity the nation's law, but he may be thankful to see the police-court missionary at hand to supplement his efforts and attempt that which is above and beyond his soke. The State can remit penalty but not forgive, for forgiveness is a personal relationship. The State can decide justly between two litigants; only the Church can reconcile them. Justice belongs to that 'nature' which 'grace' presupposes and transcends; the Church, therefore, is not unconcerned with justice, but justice is the sphere of the State, redemption of the Church. Church and State for all these reasons must proceed together—not as a tandem but in double harness.

The State is concerned with music, letters, painting, architecture, drama and religion, but its sovereignty does not extend to these. It may endow art galleries, orchestras, municipal theatres, literary institutes and Universities as part of its provision for the good life of the citizens, but State control of the arts is destructive of all art. Yesterday Sibelius was banned in Finland; to-day Chopin may not be played in Poland. The case of religion is the same. How far the State should endow or 'establish' religion is a matter of expediency as it is of dispute, but only as it is free can the Church perform its true service for the State.

Art, music and letters are human interests that must be autonomous; their development must be left to voluntary initiative and interest. Is the Church, then, a voluntary association like a school of art or letters? From the point of view of politics it must be so, from the point of view of religion it cannot be. Many men of taste, who are sympathetically disposed to the Christian faith in general, are conscious of a strong aversion from the Christian Church. They would doubtless think more kindly of it, if only it would die. When people are dead and have ceased by dying to exasperate and intimidate and thwart us, we can often see them far more clearly than when we had to live with them or put up with the annoyance of their public existence. When they are gone, we have an inkling of what they really felt and meant and attempted, of 'all I could never be, all men ignored in me'. If only the Christian Church would die, even the Secularist Press would give it a good obituary notice. But, while it continues to live, it is the most heart-breaking institution on earth, by turns worldly, tyrannical, sectarian, grasping and apt to fiddle ceremoniously or sentientally while Rome (or London) burns. Christians themselves are more poignantly aware of this than are the pagans. It was Dostoievski who drew the picture of the Grand Inquisitor to hold the mirror to the Church's face. Stupidity, vulgarity, narrowness, fanaticism and disloyalty are usually far more in evidence than the boasted attributes of unity and holiness and catholicity. But, when men of taste or moral enthusiasm turn away from the Church in stupefied despair or even in disgust, 'behold, she answers with the legion of her saints'.

This book, limited to the field of 'natural theology', dare not enter upon the supernatural claims of the Church nor even attempt a theological definition. For our present purpose the Church is a society or group of societies which exist to worship God, to witness to the ideal and commend it by example. Such an institution is necessary for moral progress and renewal. Virtue is always praised; the heaviest charge levelled by the world against the Church is simply that it is not Christian. Christ is the measure of man's duty. Dr. William Paton tells of a Hindu boy who said to a Christian missionary, 'You know, sir, it is our Christian duty to love our Mohammedan brethren'. No one objects to Christians being Christlike; on the other hand, there is apt to be tension between the idealists and the practical, between the demands of justice and the ministries of redemption, between the conscientious minority and the easy-going crowd. The British, after their kind, have achieved a compromise that 'works'. The State excuses the parsons from conscription and service on juries, appoints chaplains to hospitals, prisons and regiments, and encourages voluntary activities of mercy which fall outside its own competence and scope. In such matters as war and criminal procedure, then, the ideal demands of religion are thus represented by the professionals; for the rest the Christians must conform to the general standards and requirements of society. With a race that is not dangerously religious the compromise works so smoothly as scarcely to be recognized as such. But morality has the attributes at once of reason and of high explosive. It is obviously to the advantage of the State that as many citizens as possible should belong to a voluntary *societas* which commits them to the pursuit of the highest morality —here the Church is the hand-maid of the State. On the other hand, what ancient or modern State could endure the Church if she were truly prophetic in word and action with regard to crying social ills?—here the Church is dynamite within the State. Christ has drawn the wonder and homage of mankind; he is man's ideal. But he was done to death by the civil and religious authorities of his time, and it may well be doubted whether any modern civilized State could endure his burning words and revolutionary demands. Even Marcus Aurelius, noblest of the pagans, was a persecutor of the Christians. If a man follows the way of humane reason, he may find it leads him to a Cross in the end; then, where reason says both yes and no, a man becomes aware that nature itself cannot be fulfilled apart from grace, that reason is not enough, and that there must be given that strengthening and illuminating Spirit from beyond which is called

Fons vivus, ignis, caritas
Et spiritalis unctio.

III

The rest of this chapter is virtually an appendix offering a personal and fallible comment upon two contemporary and urgent problems.

It is for the Church to testify to the ideal but not to seek to impose it on the State. So far as possible statute law must reflect the ideal or eternal law, but, since law far in advance of public opinion is ineffectual and even brings the idea of law in disrepute, statute law can only be an approximation to ideal justice. This may be illustrated by reference to the laws relating to marriage and divorce. Canon 1118 of the Roman Codex lays it down that marriage is indissoluble—*matrimonium validum ratum et consummatum nulla potestate humana nullaque causa, praeterquam morte, dissolvi potest.* A famous encyclical of Pope Pius VI, *Casti Connubii*, thus expounds the principle: 'Marriage even in the state of nature and certainly long before it was raised to the dignity of a sacrament was divinely instituted in such a way that it should carry with it a perpetual and indissoluble bond which cannot therefore be dissolved by any civil law.' Wherever it has the power, therefore, the Roman Church opposes and prevents the legal recognition of divorce under any circumstances whatsoever.

It is to be thought that the Pope was not speaking with his usual precision on this occasion, for it appears that he does not distinguish between the indissolubility and what has been called the indissolvendibility of marriage, that is, between the propositions, 'the marriage bond can never be broken', and 'the marriage bond ought never to be broken', between a judgement of fact and a judgement of duty. Marriage is not indissoluble, for, whether it be viewed physically or spiritually, it is a bond that is broken in many examples. Indeed, regarded as a spiritual bond, marriage is much more clearly dissolved by discord than by death.

But the indissolvendibility of marriage, if the term be permitted, may be regarded as a law of nature and therefore of nature's great Original. Like the family itself, marriage is an institution at once natural and divinely given; it is intended by nature to be permanent, for without the permanence of the marriage bond there can be no stability for family life. The mutual fidelity of husband and wife is intended by nature and may properly be demanded by the Church, whose sphere is the ideal. But nature herself often falls short of her purposes, producing inferior specimens of this and that; and evidence grows from year to year that the marriage bond is not indissoluble, whether the law recognize the fact or not. Indeed, it is taught by many Christians that sacramental grace is needed for the keeping of the marriage vows, so that nature would appear to demand that which is beyond nature; and it cannot well be maintained that no civil law can dissolve marriage, when there can be shown the contrary example and authority of Moses himself. Were it literally true that marriage is indissoluble, divorce would be no more than the innocuous recognition of an event that had not occurred. It seems wiser to suppose that divorce, like war, is always a 'breach in nature', but that under certain circumstances it may be the lesser of two evils. In any case there is a distinction between the moral standards which the Church may impose upon its members and those which the State can enforce upon all citizens.

The extreme intransigeance of the Roman Church in this matter is due to loyalty to the teaching of Christ in the New Testament. But it is a matter of dispute whether that teaching has been rightly understood. Our Lord undoubtedly declared the indissolubility of marriage to be according to the will of God; husband and wife may not separate and remarry under any circumstances. He who so spoke is *rex et legifer noster*. But it would seem to many that he here spoke as Prophet, not as Law-giver. He seems to have implied that the marriage bond could be broken—*non debet dissolvi*, not *non potest*—and that man could separate that which God had joined together. His words ordain not what is to be done if the marriage bond be broken, but only that it should not be broken. Or, if he here was Lawgiver, it was as concerned with his new Kingdom, not with the duties of secular governments. If men remained 'under the law' and did not enter 'into grace', to use St. Paul's phraseology, Moses' legislation 'for the hardness of men's hearts' would presumably be valid still.

Church and State contemplate one and the same human nature and stand for the same ideals. The indissolubility of the marriage state is the will of God and the law of nature; to this, therefore, the statute law of the land must approximate so far as circumstances will permit. The Church may enforce upon her members rules which are far closer to the ideal, but even the Church cannot prevent the marriage bond from being broken. In a letter to *The Times* of 17th February 1937, Professor T. W. Manson admirably summed up this aspect of the question: 'the positive teaching of our Lord on the subject of marriage . . . quite clearly holds up the ideal of a life-long union. That ideal is binding upon the conscience of all who profess themselves Christians. They can neither reduce it nor evade it; and it would seem to be the plain duty of the Church to maintain this ideal within its own borders, and—

following the example of our Lord—to state plainly where and how legal provisions holding outside the Church come short of the Christian ideal.' Both Church and State have to deal with many failures due to human frailty; they may properly agree in opinion and aim, yet differ in judicial sentence. But, sovereign *in suo ordine*, the Church exceeds her office when, passing beyond exhortation and example to command, she seeks to dictate the legislation of the State.

IV

'A nation's system of education', writes Mr. T. S. Eliot, 'is much more important than its system of government.' Family and Church and State are alike vitally interested in education. Fruitful collaboration has been hindered in England, the real issues almost obscured, and the concern of parents and teachers largely disregarded because of the miserable bickerings of the Christian sects about 'religious teaching in the schools'.

Both 'Council Schools' and 'Church Schools' are provided for the elementary instruction of the poor in the very curious and snobbish system of English education. There are those who in sentiment and imagination place at the heart of every village in England the Church, the public-house, the school. This last is conceived as the annex of the Church; the parson should have a general oversight of all its activities; the teachers should without exception be communicant members of the parish church, and, in view of the 'sacrifices' made (before or after death) by the wealthy deceased, the State should support the school and pay the teachers. No criticism can be made of this scheme except inapplicability to the present religious situation in the country. Both Roman Catholics and Dissenters are now very numerous. The Roman Catholics demand separate schools for their members and have shown themselves willing to give of their own substance as well as to receive State subventions for such schools. But the Dissenters, who suffer no impulse to provide schools of their own and have a proper distaste for sectarian education, take great exception to the Anglican monopoly in many schools supported in the main by the exactions of the rate-collector. They say that religious tests should have no place in the nation's schools, and that the exclusion of Free Church teachers from any State schools is a manifest injustice; they object to the ecclesiastical atmosphere of the so-called 'Church schools' and to the religious teaching given there. They demand what they call undenominational teaching in the nation's schools.

Both Anglicans and Nonconformists have a case. All non-Anglican teachers have a grievance that many appointments are closed to them in the national system of education on no other ground than that they do not belong to the local vicar's flock. Furthermore, such has been the varied theological training in the Anglican Church in years past that there have been parsons whose ideas of theology and of the doctrines suitable for the instruction of the young were limited to the prejudices of their own ecclesiastical party and tended to be sectarian in proportion as they assumed the name of 'Catholic'. Free Church parents naturally object to having their children taught variegations of doctrine which would horrify the bench of bishops almost as much as they offend the good sense of other Christian persuasions. Even more frequent cause of offence has been the enthusiasm for 'Church' schools as against Council schools which has betrayed certain of the clergy and their friends into what their opponents deem political intrigue. But there is, or there ought to be, no genuine difficulty about the substance of religious teaching. The local school must be distinguished from a Confirmation class, and Free Churchmen who proudly send their sons to the Anglican Public Schools as soon as they can afford the fees have never quarrelled with the religious teaching given there. Many counties now, and pre-eminently Cambridgeshire, have an agreed syllabus of religious instruction which is satisfactory to the men of reason and sober conviction on both sides.

Up to a point, then, Free Churchmen have made out their case, but they are much to blame in so far as they have thought of religious instruction in terms of a single set of lessons insinuated, subject to a conscience clause, into the curriculum, and in their unbalanced stress upon the war-cry of No Tests for Teachers. Anglicans rightly contend that the strictly religious instruction is of little avail unless the whole curriculum and atmosphere of the school be religious. If only they be concerned that it should be Christian rather than that it should be ancillary to their proprietary brand of Christianity, a friendly arrangement becomes possible. Again, there always are, and there always must be, tests for teachers. Tests of character are not less important in the appointment of teachers than in the appointment of clerks and cashiers, nor should we be treating unfairly some man of gloomy outlook and erratic moral enthusiasms if we said to him, 'We will buy our bacon from you, or even read your books, but we will not appoint you to teach and influence our children.' Objection should be taken only to tests that are purely sectarian and not in any real sense religious. This whole wretched dispute, crippling to educational efficiency and gravely prejudicing the vital elements of instruction in the national schools, could be settled now, and there seems at last a reasonable hope that the men of humanity and understanding may be given the chance to promulgate a scheme.

Meanwhile, the vital issue is overlooked. There is, and there can be, no such thing as religiously neutral education. Education must be in the broad sense religious or irreligious. If it does not inculcate a Christian outlook, it will inculcate a materialist or a Communist or a nationalist or Nazi outlook. We may not ask the national schools to teach theology, but history and reason demand that in the broad sense our schools should be Christian. This is only in very small degree a matter of definite religious instruction. 'Education', says Mr. T. S. Eliot again, 'must be something more than the acquisition of information, technical competence, or superficial culture.' The State is concerned with education as a training for the duties of a citizen. The inspiration and goal of education must be the nation's spiritual inheritance and the 'philosophy' which is the foundation of the national life and unity. There is no reason why distinctively Christian doctrine should not be taught in national schools where such teaching is acceptable to the vast majority of the parents, but the teaching of Christian doctrine is not the duty of the State but of the Church. The State, however, should be concerned (by no means less for its secondary than for its primary schools) that the children should 'fear God and honour the king', that they should recognize and reverence the eternal law of justice, that they should be taught ideals of self-restraint, of service and of mercy, that they should know Shakespeare and the Bible as part of the moral and spiritual inheritance of their native land. This is not a question of 'undenominational' teaching, but of the principles of 'natural theology' which concern the State as such and are the presupposition of the further teaching of the Church. The basis of religious education must obviously be the Bible. It is certainly impossible to distinguish sharply between that in the Bible which is distinctively Christian and that which appeals to reason and conscience apart from supernatural faith. But who should desire to draw a hard and fast line? Let the Bible be taught by those who reverence and love it, and let the rest be left to home and Church.

Education is a field where Church and State very clearly

must co-operate. It sufficiently illustrates the two principles that it is not the task of the State to teach the Christian faith, but that religion is a vital concern of the State as such. There is in the long run no ultimate religious neutrality possible for the State. Either it will be materialist or Nazi or Christian; but that which is here called Christian is in the sphere of natural theology, of 'pauser reason' and of conscience.

CODA

multi thyrsigeri, pauci Bacchi.

A VERY singular vision is recorded in the seventh chapter of the Book of Daniel. 'I saw in my vision by night', says the seer, 'and, behold, the four winds of the heaven strove upon the great sea.' Out of this troubled sea arises a series of strange heraldic beasts representing the great heathen empires of antiquity. Presently there comes, not from the sea but from heaven, 'one like a Man' who represents a humane or human empire that is also the Kingdom of God. In a ponderous and pedestrian manner my book has followed the same course. The political progeny of Hobbes and of Rousseau, of Marx and of Hitler, owns kinship with the monstrous brood of Daniel's vision. Rejecting them as inhuman I have sketched in bare outline a pleasanter conception of society, rational and moral, humane and Christian. So far I conceive myself to have carried with me (in the main) the persevering and the patient amongst the readers whom most I have in mind. Decent, honourable, just and kindly men will agree with me in general.

But a writer must deal honestly by those who do him the courtesy of reading through his pages. I must go manfully to my conclusion, though it give offence. I said in my preface, first, that every political problem is at bottom theological, and, second, that no political doctrine has prevailing power unless it be allied to a religion or pseudo-religion of some sort. The view I have propounded with a laudable absence of originality is reasonable, respectable, the very apogee of common sense, but it will remain ineffectual, unappealing and helpless before the fierce fanaticisms of Moscow and Berchtesgaden, unless it be allied to the enthusiasms of a virile and a passionate faith.

It might seem futile (however logical) to conclude that, if my contemplated reader would serve his country and humanity, he must become much more acutely and impressively religious; for unhappily man's inability to hoist himself by his own waist-band has its parallel in the sphere of religion. Natural theology is common sense, but its ideas only catch fire as they are assumed into the revelation of the holy will of the living God. Faith is, I believe, a supernatural gift of God; we may desire it, or we may fear it, but of ourselves we cannot compass it.

But at least we can see that Reason points towards it and needs it for its own fulfilment. For the most part this book has kept strictly to 'natural theology' and to Reason. But more than once we have found ourselves upon the edge of a contradiction, if Reason cannot point or pass beyond itself. I suggested, for instance, that monogamy and conjugal fidelity is a 'natural law', yet experience proves that in many cases it is altogether beyond unaided human nature. Again, I said that the Christlike man is everywhere respected and honoured by his fellows; on the other hand, as Plato himself foresaw, the perfectly just man will inevitably in a world like this be crucified. Nature, it might seem, compels us to that which is in itself impossible; we must destroy that which we love. This inherent contradiction springs from the divided or, as the theologians say, the 'fallen' state of human nature. He who, taking an optimistic view of human nature, regards it as wholly good apart from convention and from circumstance is a sentimentalist whose political constructions lead first to anarchy and then to tyranny. He who takes a pessimistic view and deems human nature to be in itself without qualification bad—

natura deleta—must despair of politics altogether. Human nature, as we know it, is both good and bad; it is *natura volnerata*, 'fallen' and yet not so fallen as to have wholly lost the image of the divine. Man is naturally good, yet assuredly 'it is not in man to direct his steps aright'. That is the paradox or dilemma of our nature.

Human nature is naturally good; that is to say, human nature is good when it is what it was meant to be. Yet no man who contemplates the world, whether he call himself theologian or not, can escape the tragic fact of human sin with its trail of unimaginable suffering and misery and hopelessness over all the world. A rational and sensible philosophy of the State is very impotent to heal the wounds of our society. Men of good-will, therefore, apart from the Gospel, feel themselves to be like shipwrecked mariners, some on flimsy rafts, some floundering in the sea, doing what they can for their neighbours but without ultimate confidence or hope. Human life is ultimately irrational unless the resolving of the discord be in God.

But here, too, is a dilemma forced upon us, not by the gratuitous speculations of the theologians, but by our inevitable reasoning. God as the Author and Sustainer of the world, apprehended or glimpsed in the marvellous beauties of nature, in the sanctities of our homes, in the high principles of reason and of conscience, in all that is sacred and sublime, must be conceived as good. He whose eternal law is righteousness must himself be righteous; he who requires justice and mercy must himself be just and merciful. But how are we to conceive his relation to the world of human aspiration and failure, nobility and shame, to a society that longs for peace and is driven by passion or by conscience into war? Is he as one standing on the beach, while men struggle and drown in the water, shouting excellent advice to them through a megaphone and reproaching them because, had they taken his advice, they would never have got into this trouble? The goodness of such a God might seem less than the goodness of a man who in such a case would venture his life to save the drowning. It would be an intolerable contradiction that men should be better or more resourceful than the God from whom all goodness is derived. If God is good, as he must be good, then it might seem that—*ingens et laetum paradoxon*—he too must 'risk his life' in coming to the rescue. Here Reason staggers and kindling faith adores.

The Christian Gospel, the catholic faith, is beyond Reason, yet it is the only Reason. It declares that in the Person of Jesus Christ Almighty God has himself plunged, as it were, into the angry sea to rescue us, that, himself with us in our weakness and despair, he has stretched out his hand to hold us and to bring us home. In the Cross of Christ we see the measure and the cost of love, in the Resurrection of Christ the promise and the pledge of victory. God has identified himself with us in our defeat, that he might identify us with himself in victory. From this apprehension arises our love for God, so far beyond a mere reverence and respect for his most holy law.

This Gospel is not irrelevant to politics. Of itself it neither involves a political theory nor offers any promise of a millennium on earth. But there are nations that owe their very existence to the Christian faith; in the love of God there is a power given whereby man can triumph over sin; and there is a new society on earth, the Christian Church. The Church from many aspects is an all too human institution, yet it carries within it the seed not only of its own renewal but also of the world's. 'The only hope for Europe', writes that well-informed observer, Mr. Richard Russell, 'appears to lie in those small communities of Christians, both Catholic and Protestant, who live in the world and who are attempting to leaven it, as the Christian Church leavened the Roman Empire.

They are the only persons whose faith remains untroubled in the bankruptcy of liberalism, the bankruptcy of nationalism, and the bankruptcy of dictatorship. Theirs is a philosophy which is untouched by the changes of the passing moment. They have fought the battle for peace in their own hearts and are the only men confident of bringing order to a distracted world. They know that God has a plan for each one of them, and they aim to work in harmony with his plan. The tide is with them, as it was with the Christian Church in the catacombs, and they know that their ark will weather the tempest.' We may have an excellent political philosophy, and yet despair of all political action. To be effective, our longing for a new and better world must be quickened and empowered by the passion of a personal loyalty to Christ and a devotion to the will of God. It is hard to keep our religious life above freezing point if we never go to church and never have family prayers at home.

It is easy and futile to say that, if only every one were Christian, 'everything in the garden would be lovely', and there would be no social and international problems. For, in the first place, a kindly disposition is no substitute for thought, and, in the second, the world will not become Christian in our life-time. But 'Christendom', as it has here been sketched, is no mere dream but practical politics if its cause be served by those who add to a sound philosophy a passionate faith. In our political thinking we have reason; do we also have religion? *Ignem sui amoris accendat Deus in cordibus nostris*—God kindle the fire of His love within our hearts!

INDEX

INDEX

INDEX

INDEX

Printed by Western Printing Services Limited, Bristol